EASY GUITAR

Taylor Swift Speak Now

ISBN 978-1-61780-360-4

HAL•LEONARD®
CORPORATION
7777 W. BLUEMOUND RD. P.O. BOX 13819 MILWAUKEE, WI 53213

Visit Hal Leonard Online at
www.halleonard.com

Mine

Words and Music by Taylor Swift

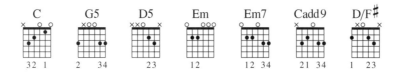

Strum Pattern: 1, 3
Pick Pattern: 3

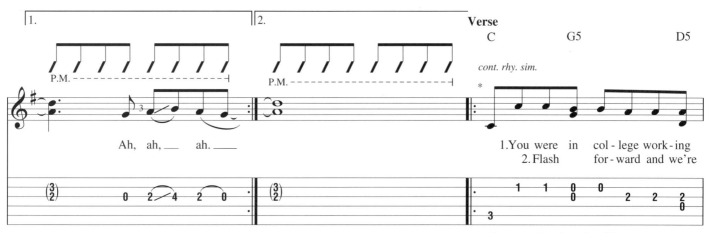

*Sung as written throughout Verse.

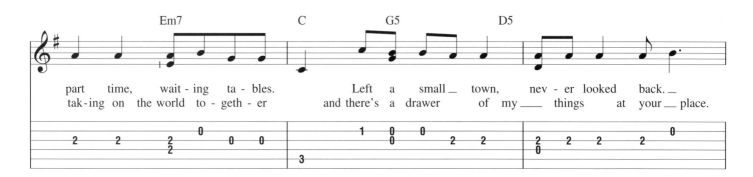

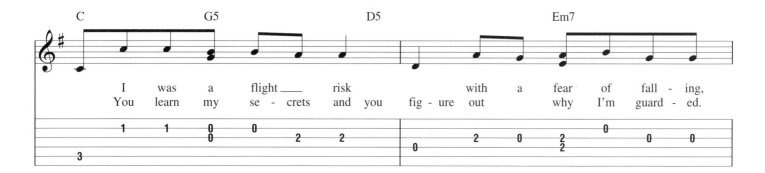

I was a flight ___ risk with a fear of fall - ing,
You learn my se - crets and you fig - ure out why I'm guard - ed.

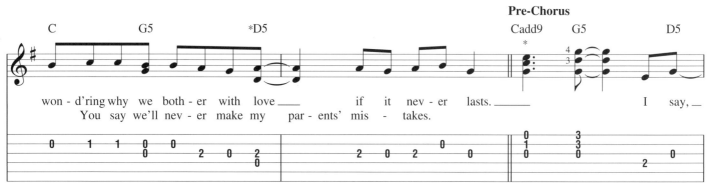

won - d'ring why we both - er with love ___ if it nev - er lasts. ___ I say, ___
You say we'll nev - er make my par - ents' mis - takes.

*Let chord ring.

Pre-Chorus

*Sung one octave higher, except where noted.

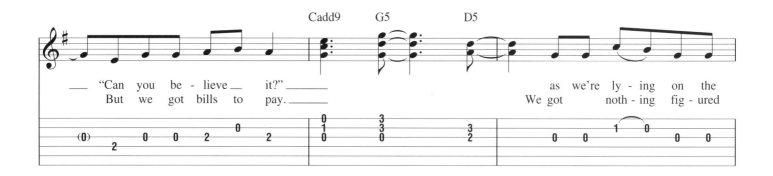

___ "Can you be - lieve ___ it?" ___ as we're ly - ing on the
But we got bills to pay. ___ We got noth - ing fig - ured

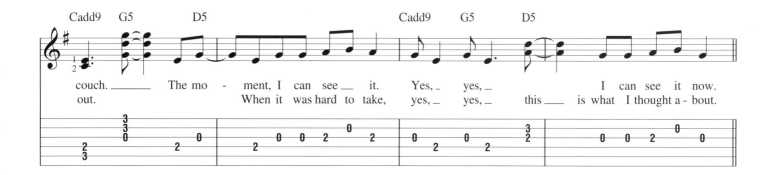

couch. ___ The mo - ment, I can see ___ it. Yes, ___ yes, ___ I can see it now.
out. When it was hard to take, yes, ___ yes, ___ this ___ is what I thought a - bout.

% Chorus

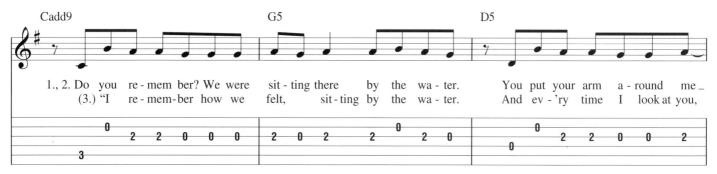

1., 2. Do you re - mem - ber? We were sit - ting there by the wa - ter. You put your arm a - round me ___
(3.) "I re - mem - ber how we felt, sit - ting by the wa - ter. And ev - 'ry time I look at you,

3

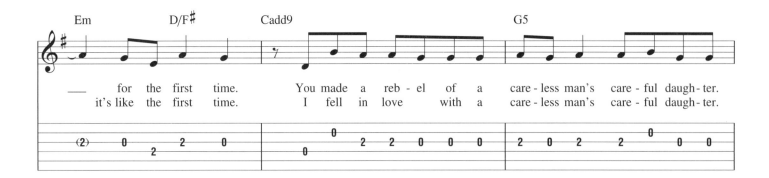

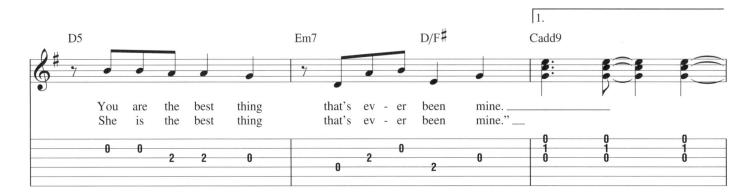

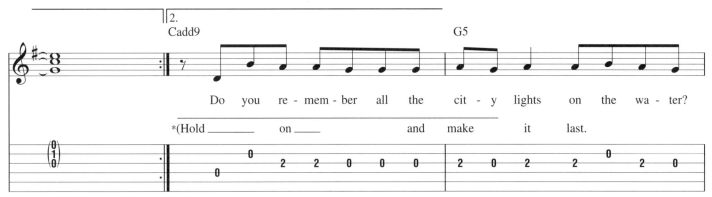

*Bkgd vocals sung 2nd time only.

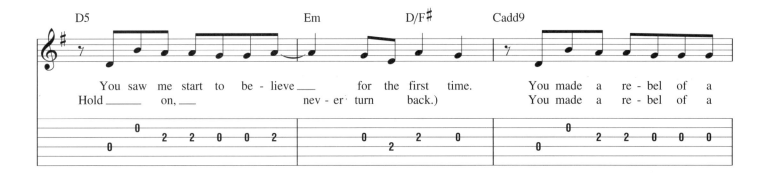

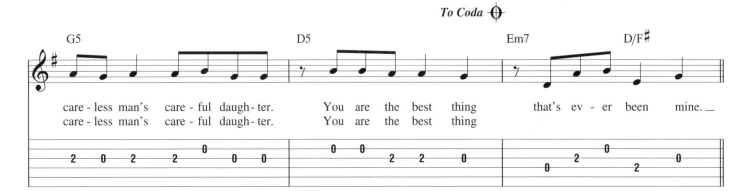

Interlude

Uh, oh, — oh. _____ And I re-

Bridge

mem - ber that fight, two - thir - ty A. M. You said ev - 'ry - thing was slip - ping right

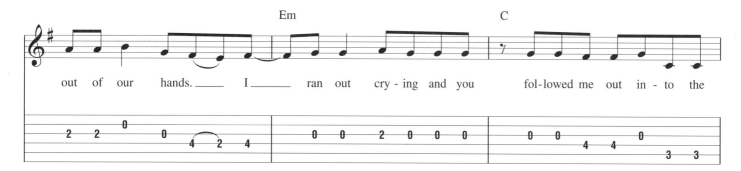

out of our hands. ___ I ___ ran out cry - ing and you fol - lowed me out in - to the

Pre-Chorus

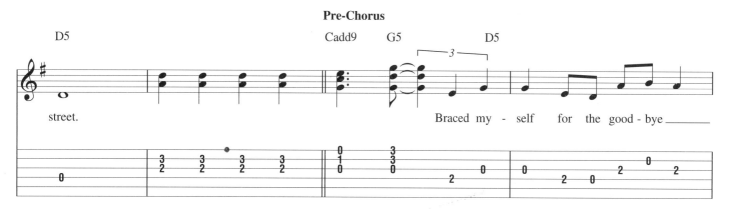

street. Braced my - self for the good - bye _____

— 'cause that's all ___ I've ev - er known. _____ And you __

5

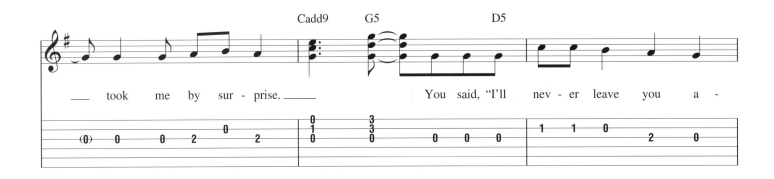

took me by sur - prise. _____ You said, "I'll nev - er leave you a -

D.S. al Coda
(take 2nd ending)

⊕ **Coda**

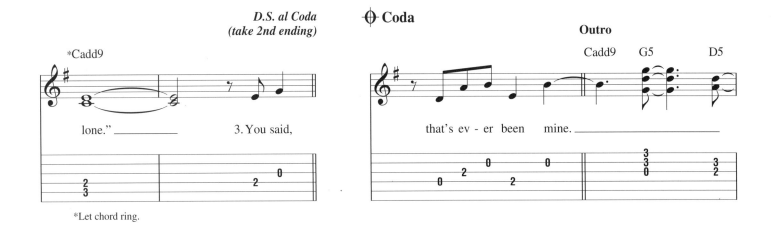

lone." _____ 3. You said,

Outro

that's ev - er been mine. _____

*Let chord ring.

Do you be - lieve it? We're gon - na make it, now.

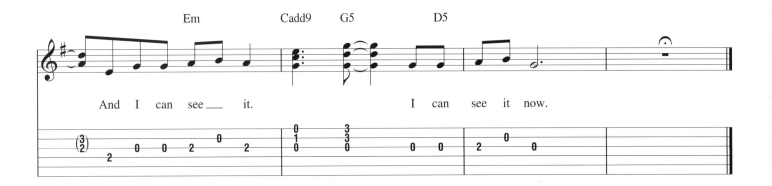

And I can see ___ it. I can see it now.

Mean

Words and Music by Taylor Swift

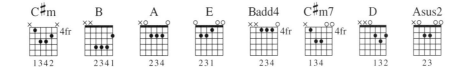

Strum Pattern: 2, 5
Pick Pattern: 1, 4

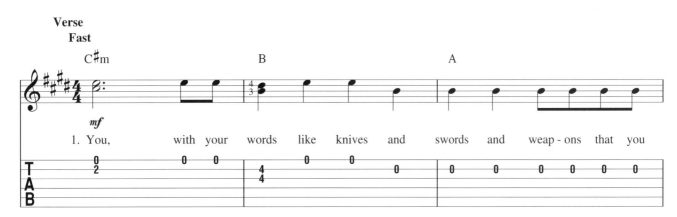

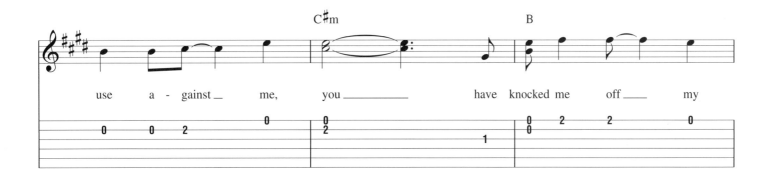

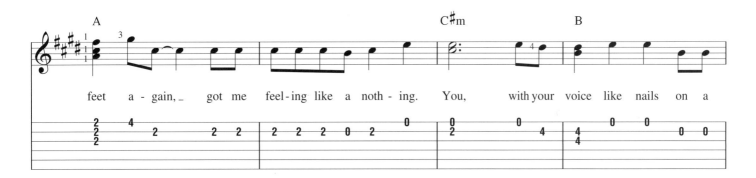

chalk - board, call - ing me out ___ when I'm wound - ed. You, pick - ing on the weak - er man. ___

Pre-Chorus

___ Well, you can take me down ___

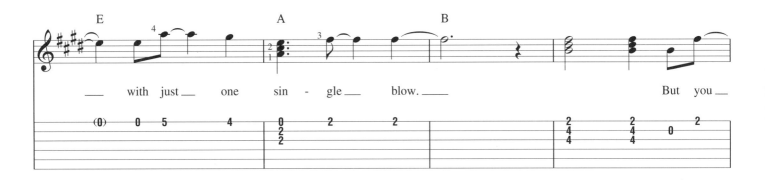

___ with just ___ one sin - gle ___ blow. ___ But you

𝄋 **Chorus**

*A

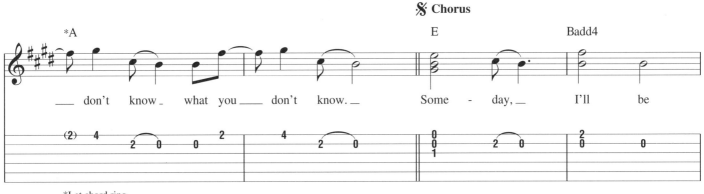

___ don't know ___ what you ___ don't know. ___ Some - day, ___ I'll be

*Let chord ring.

liv - in' in a big ol' cit - y, ___ and all you're ___ ev - er gon - na be is

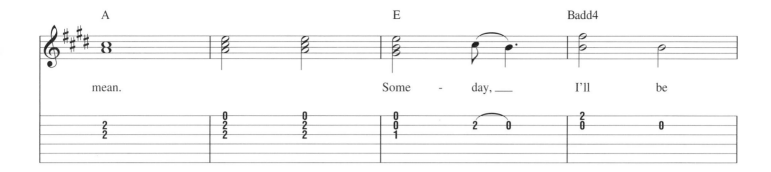

Interlude

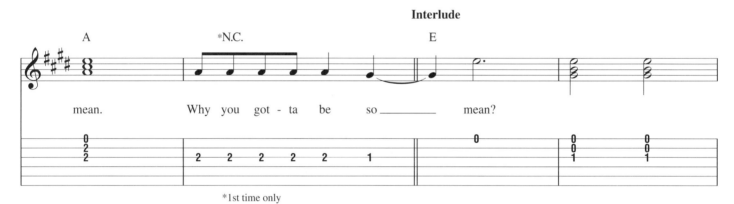

*1st time only

To Coda ⊕

Verse

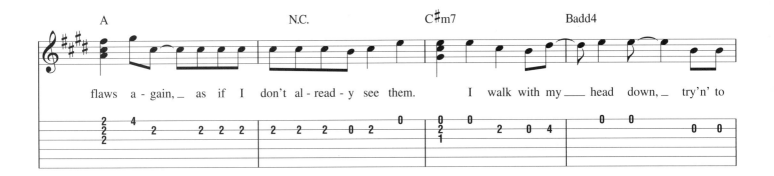

flaws a - gain, __ as if I don't al - read - y see them. I walk with my __ head down, __ try'n' to

block you out 'cause I'll nev - er im - press you. I just wan - na feel __ o -

Interlude

kay a - gain. __ I'll bet you got pushed a - round, _____

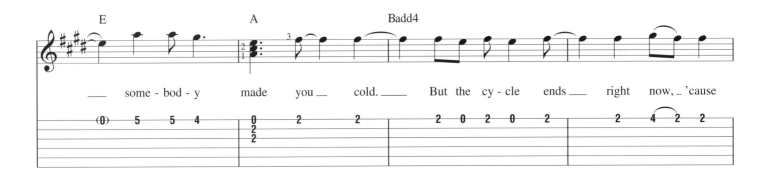

__ some - bod - y made you __ cold. __ But the cy - cle ends __ right now, __ 'cause

D.S. al Coda

you can't lead __ me down __ that road __ and you __ don't know __ what you __ don't know. __

Coda

Interlude

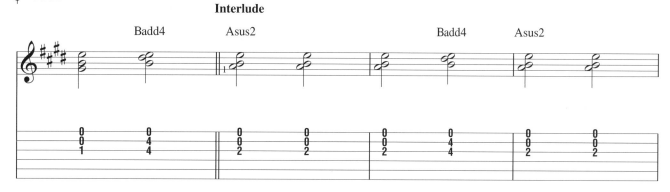

Bridge

And I ___ can see you years ___ from now ___ in a bar, talk-ing o-ver a

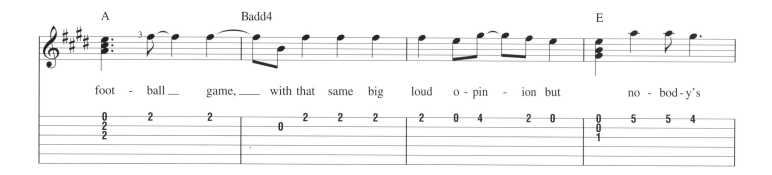

foot - ball ___ game, ___ with that same big loud o - pin - ion but no - bod-y's

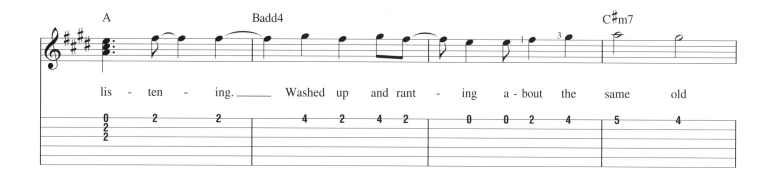

lis - ten - ing. ___ Washed up and rant - ing a-bout the same old

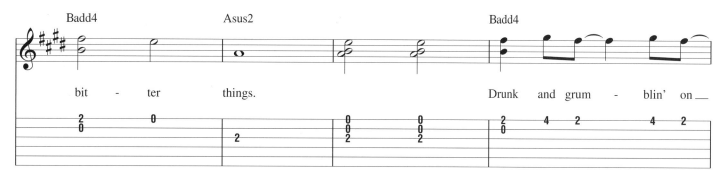

bit - ter things. Drunk and grum - blin' on ___

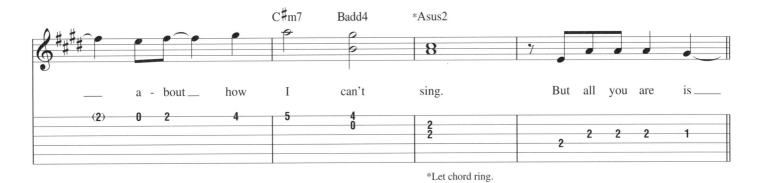

C#m7　Badd4　*Asus2

— a - bout — how I can't sing. But all you are is —

*Let chord ring.

Interlude

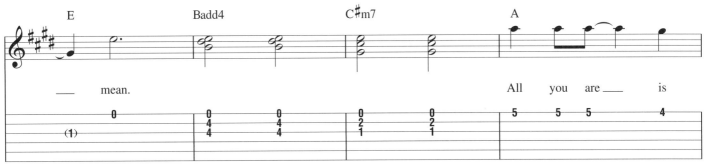

E　Badd4　C#m7　A

— mean. All you are — is

E　Badd4　C#m7　A

mean, and a li - ar, ——— and pa - thet - ic, ——— and a - lone in life, — and

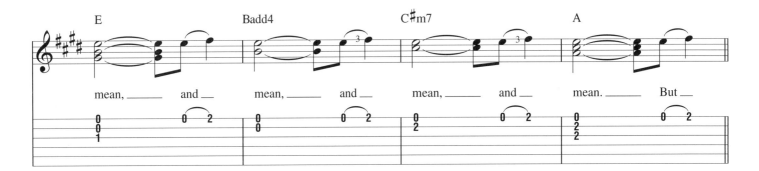

E　Badd4　C#m7　A

mean, ——— and — mean, ——— and — mean, ——— and — mean. ——— But —

Chorus

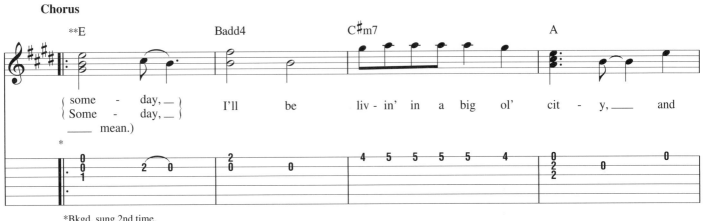

**E　Badd4　C#m7　A

{ some - day, — }
{ Some - day, — }
—— mean.)

I'll be liv - in' in a big ol' cit - y, ——— and

*Bkgd. sung 2nd time.
**1st time, N.C., next 8 meas.

12

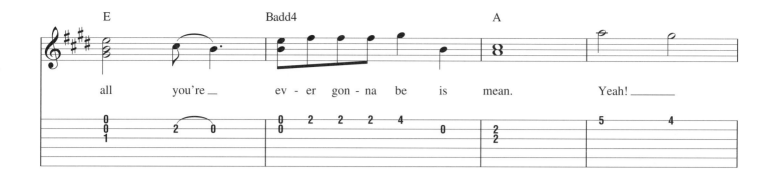

all you're ___ ev - er gon - na be is mean. Yeah! _____

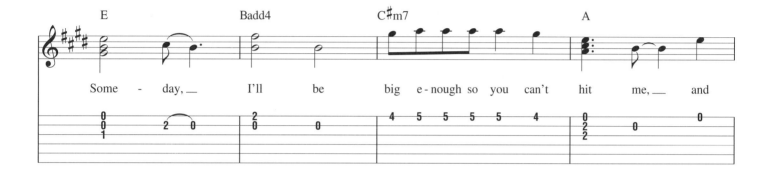

Some - day, ___ I'll be big e - nough so you can't hit me, ___ and

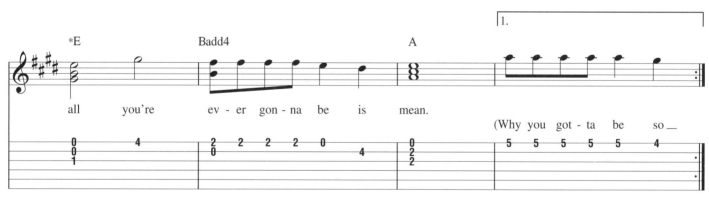

all you're ev - er gon - na be is mean.

(Why you got - ta be so ___

*2nd time, let chords ring till end.

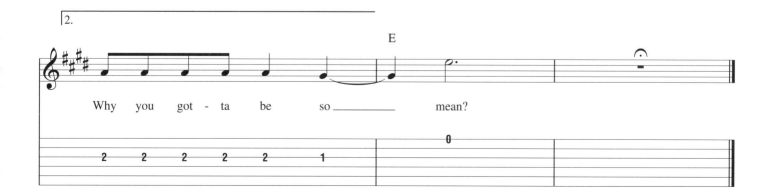

Why you got - ta be so _____ mean?

Sparks Fly

Words and Music by Taylor Swift

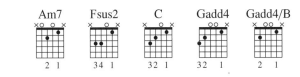

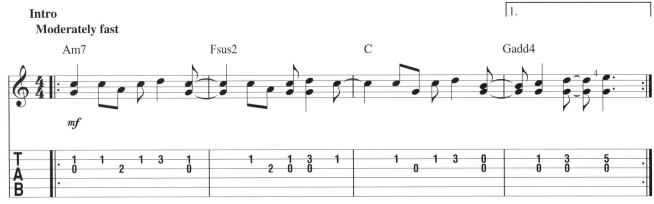

*Capo V

Strum Pattern: 1, 2
Pick Pattern: 4

Intro
Moderately fast

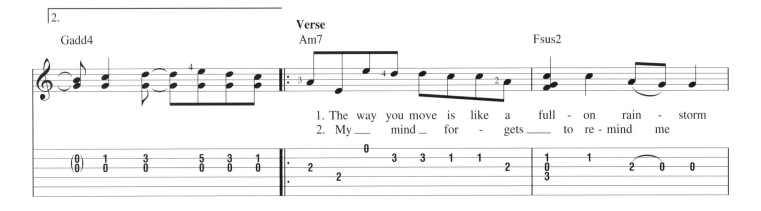

*Optional: To match recording, place capo at 5th fret.

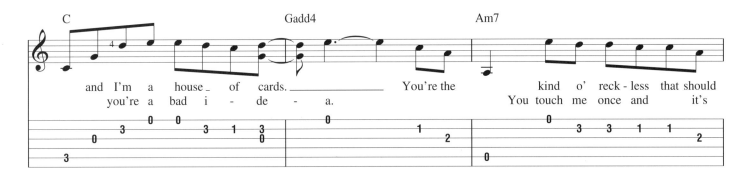

1. The way you move is like a full - on rain - storm
2. My __ mind __ for - gets __ to re - mind me

and I'm a house __ of cards. __ You're the
you're a bad i - de - a.

kind o' reck - less that should
You touch me once and it's

send me run - nin' but I kind o' know __ that I won't get far. __
real - ly some- thin', you find __ I'm e - ven bet - ter than you im - ag - ined I would be.

Pre-Chorus

And you stood there in front of me just close e-nough to touch,
I'm on my guard for the rest of the world, but with you, I know it's no

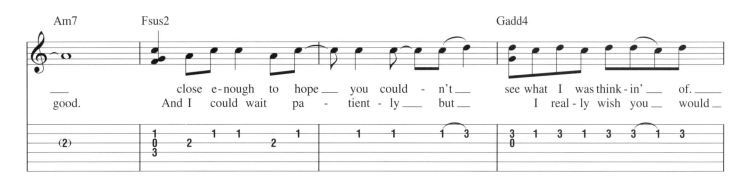

good. close e-nough to hope you could-n't see what I was think-in' of.
And I could wait pa - tient-ly but I real-ly wish you would

% Chorus

Drop ev-'ry-thing now. Meet me in the pour-ing rain.
drop ev-'ry-thing Kiss me on the side-walk,

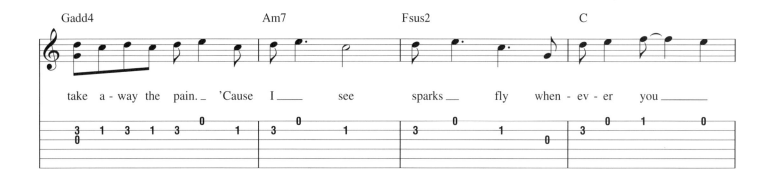

take a-way the pain. 'Cause I see sparks fly when-ev-er you

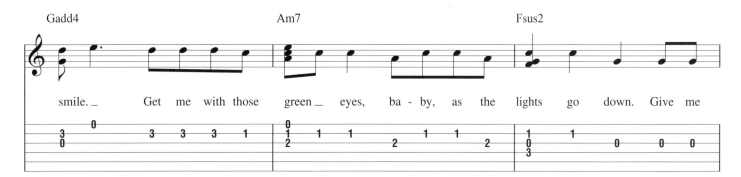

smile. Get me with those green eyes, ba-by, as the lights go down. Give me

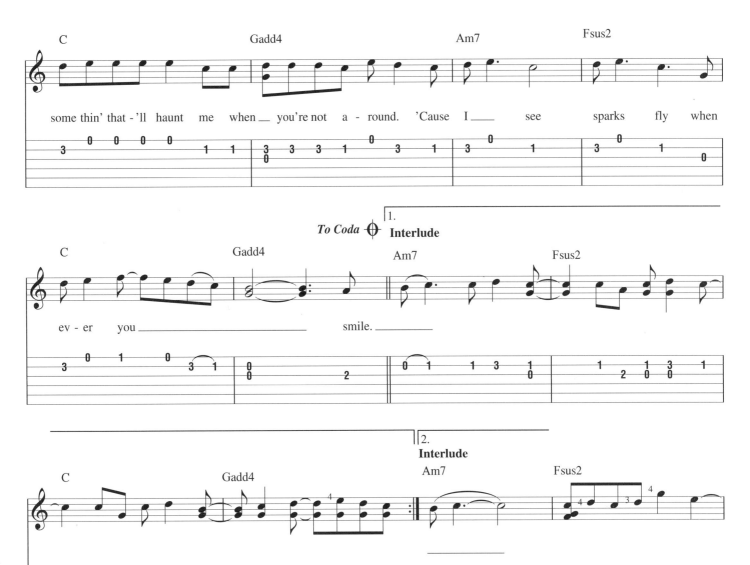

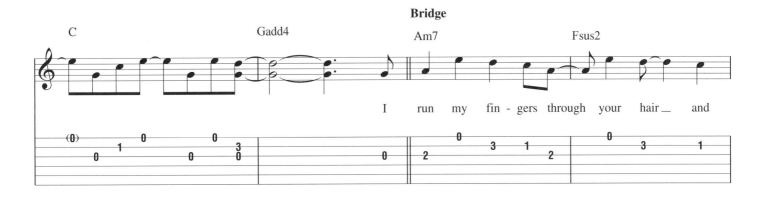

wrong e-nough to make it feel __ right. __ And lead me up the stair - case, won't you

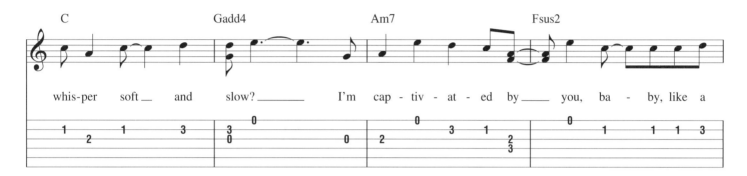

whis-per soft __ and slow? _____ I'm cap - tiv - at - ed by ___ you, ba - by, like a

D.S. al Coda   **Coda**

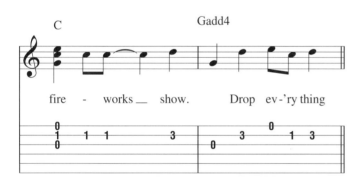

fire - works __ show. Drop ev-'ry thing

Outro
w/ Voc. ad lib.

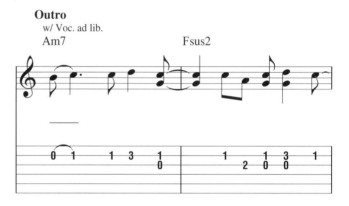

Back to December

Words and Music by Taylor Swift

*Capo II

Strum Pattern: 1
Pick Pattern: 5

Intro
Moderately, in 2

*Optional: To match recording, place capo at 2nd fret.
**Ukulele arr. for gtr., next 5 meas.

Verse

1. I'm so glad you made time to see me. How's life?
2. *See additional lyrics*

Tell me, how's your fam - 'ly? I have - n't seen ____ them in ____ a

while. ____ You've been good,

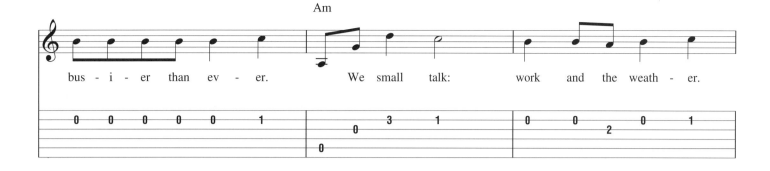

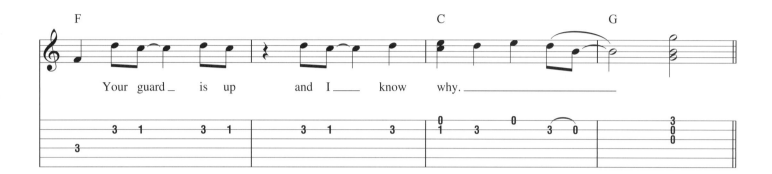

Pre-Chorus

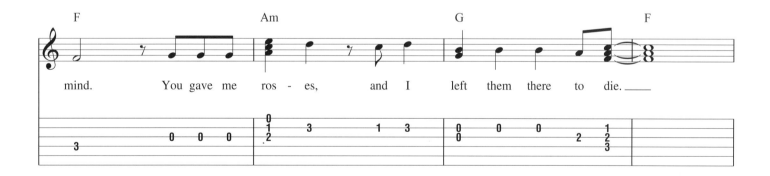

𝄋 Chorus

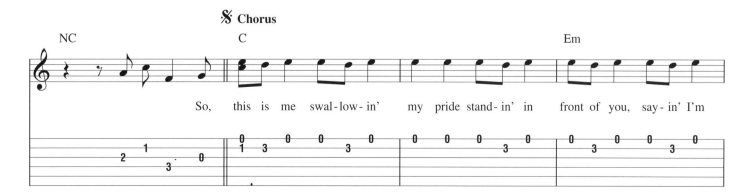

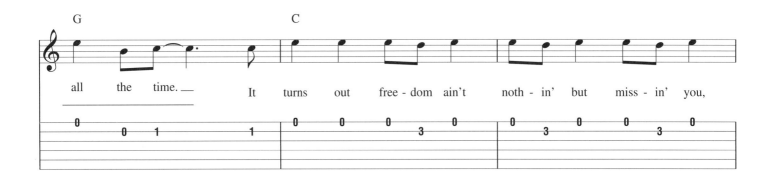

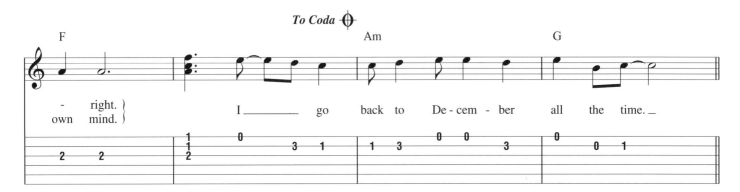

Interlude

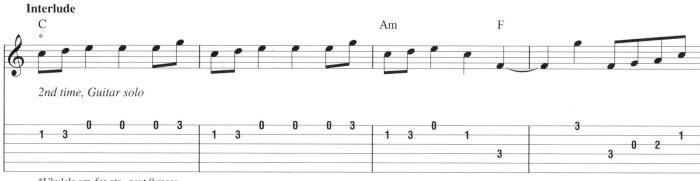

2nd time, Guitar solo

*Ukulele arr. for gtr., next 9 meas.

I miss __ your

Bridge

tan skin, ___ your sweet smile, __ so good to me, ___ so

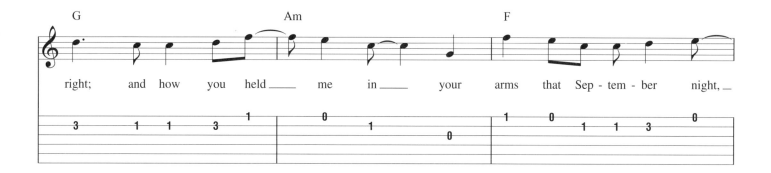

right; and how you held ___ me in ___ your arms that Sep - tem - ber night, __

___ the first time you ev - er saw __ me cry. May - be this is wish - ful think - in',

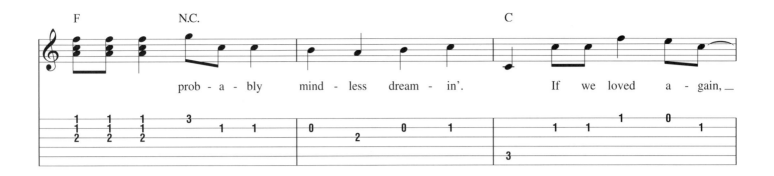

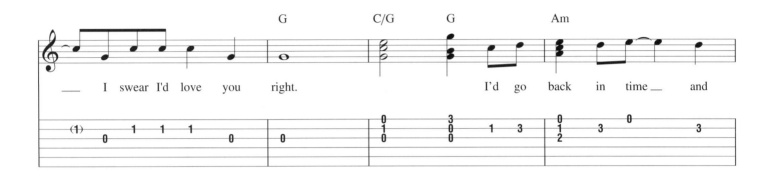

D.S. al Coda

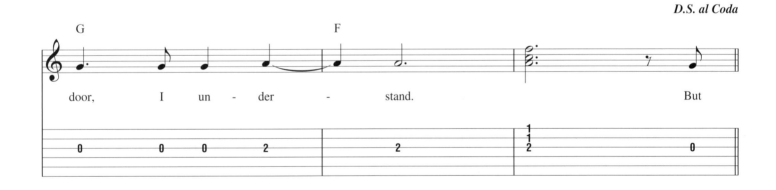

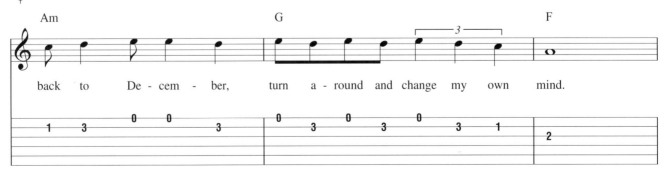

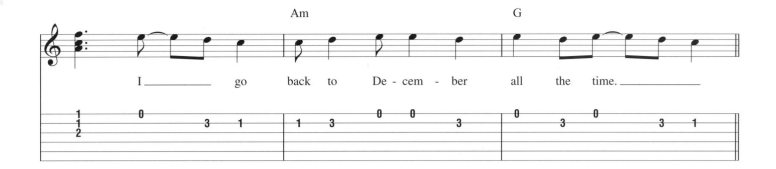

I _____ go back to De- cem- ber all the time. _____

Outro

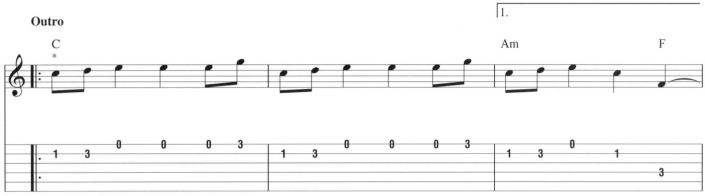

*Ukulele arr. for gtr., next 6 meas.

All the time. __

**Tie into beat 1 on repeat.

Additional Lyrics

2. These days, I haven't been sleepin';
   Stayin' up, playin' back myself leavin',
   When your birthday passed and I didn't call.
   Then I think about summer, all the beautiful times,
   I watched you laughin' from the passenger side
   And realized I loved you in the fall.

Pre-Chorus And then the cold came,
   The dark days when fear crept into my mind.
   You gave me all your love,
   And all I gave you was goodbye.

Speak Now

Words and Music by Taylor Swift

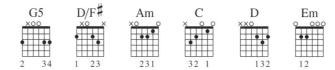

Strum Pattern: 6
Pick Pattern: 6

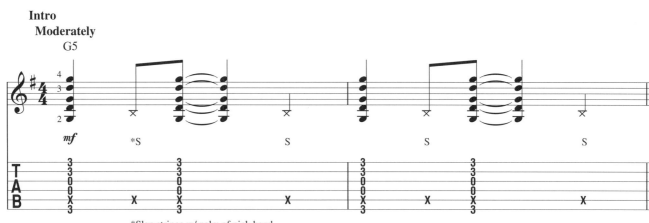

*Slap strings w/ palm of pick hand.

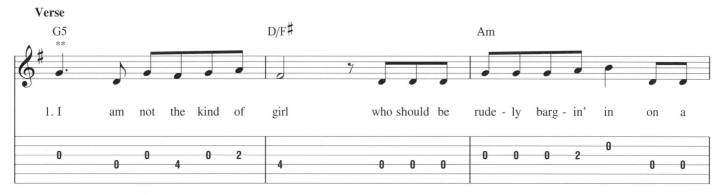

**Sung one octave higher throughout.

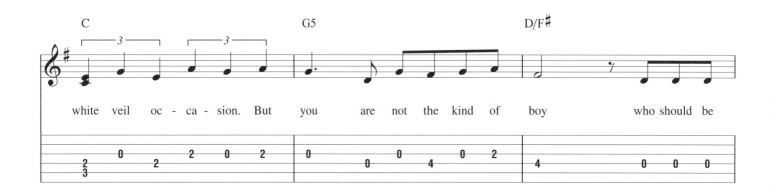

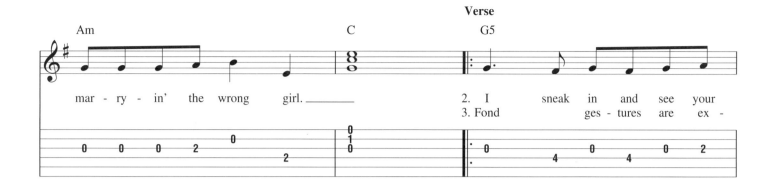

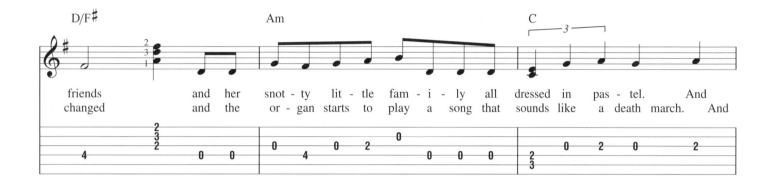

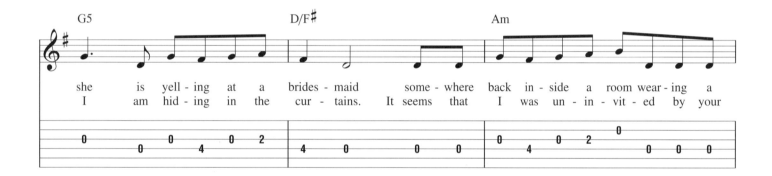

Pre-Chorus

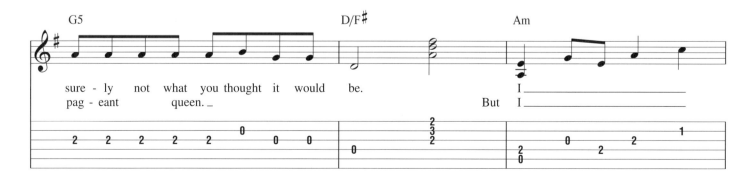

C · D · N.C.

lose my-self in a day-dream where I stand ___ and ___ say:
know ___ you wish it was me. ___ You wish it was me, ___ don't you?

 Chorus

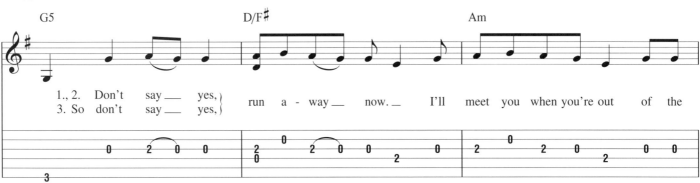

G5 · D/F# · Am

1., 2. Don't say ___ yes, }
3. So don't say ___ yes, } run a-way ___ now. ___ I'll meet you when you're out of the

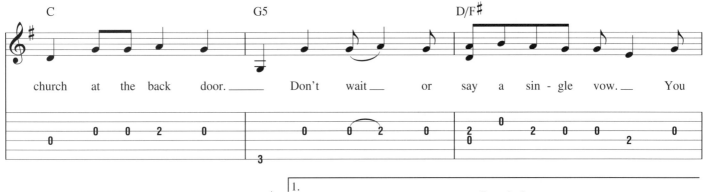

C · G5 · D/F#

church at the back door. ___ Don't wait ___ or say a sin-gle vow. ___ You

To Coda ⊕ | 1. | **Interlude**

Am · C N.C. · G5

need to hear me out. And they said, "Speak now." ___

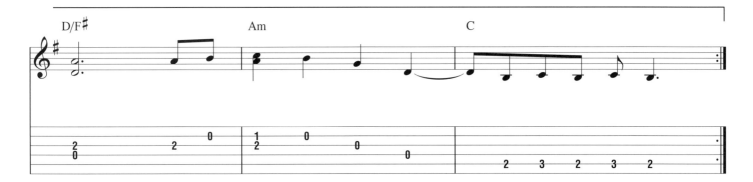

D/F# · Am · C

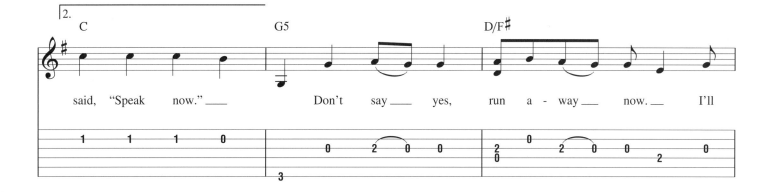

said, "Speak now." ___ Don't say ___ yes, run a-way ___ now. ___ I'll

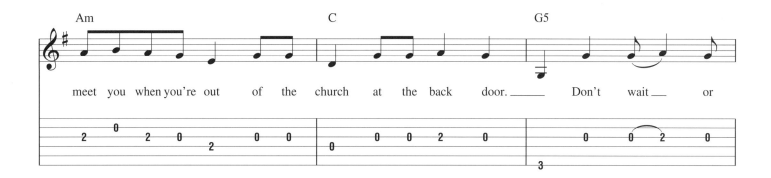

meet you when you're out of the church at the back door. ___ Don't wait ___ or

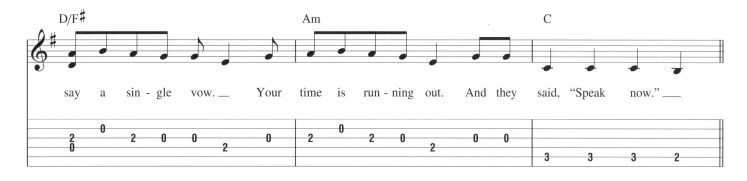

say a sin-gle vow. ___ Your time is run-ning out. And they said, "Speak now." ___

Interlude
w/ Voc. ad lib.

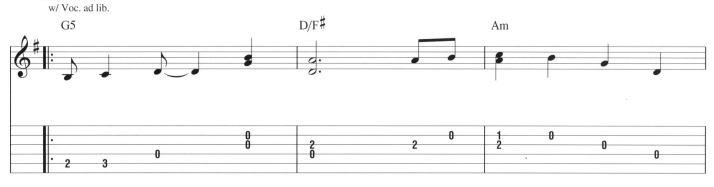

Bridge

I hear the preach-er say, "Speak now or for-ev-er

*Let chords ring, next 4 meas.

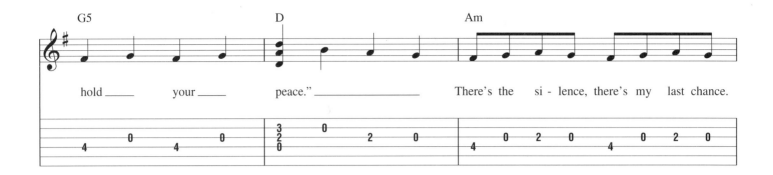

hold _____ your _____ peace." _____ There's the si - lence, there's my last chance.

I stand up with shak - y hands, all eyes on me.

*Let chord ring.

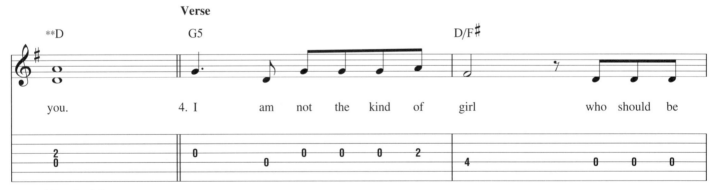

Hor - ri - fied looks from ev -'ry - one in the room but I'm on - ly look - in' at _____

Verse

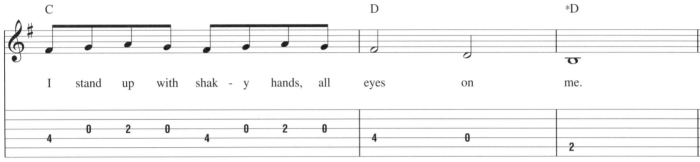

you. 4. I am not the kind of girl who should be

**Let chord ring.

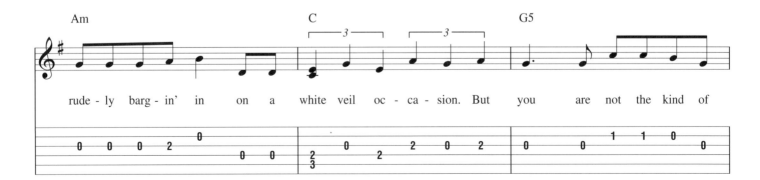

rude - ly barg - in' in on a white veil oc - ca - sion. But you are not the kind of

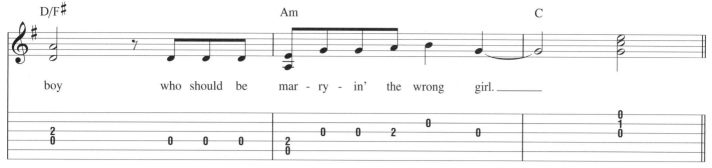

boy   who should be   mar - ry - in' the wrong   girl. _____

Coda

said, "Speak   now." ___   And you say,   "Let's run a - way ___ now. ___   I'll

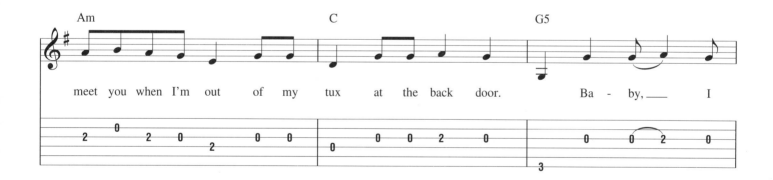

meet you when I'm out of my tux at the back door.   Ba - by, ___   I

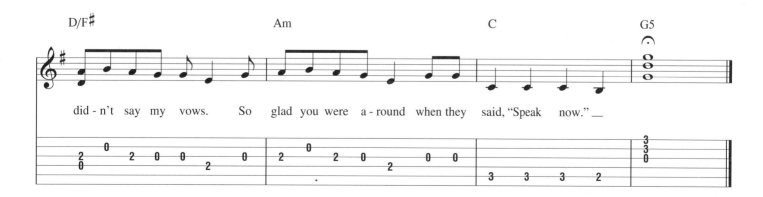

did - n't say my vows.   So glad you were a - round when they said, "Speak now." ___

Dear John

Words and Music by Taylor Swift

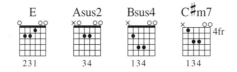

Strum Pattern: 9
Pick Pattern: 7

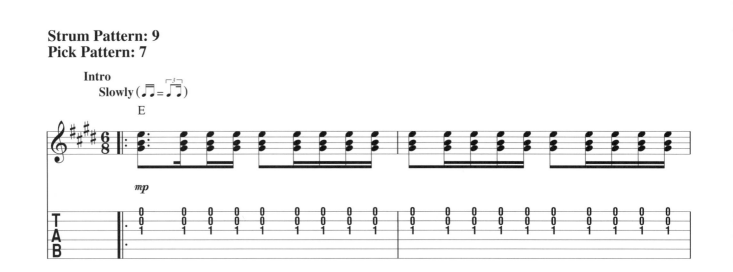

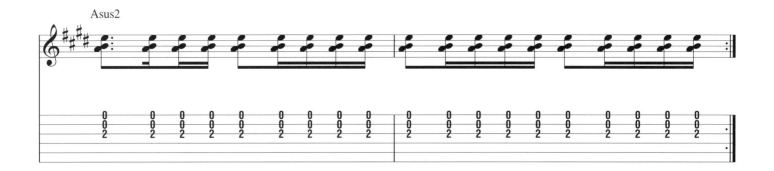

Verse

1. Long were the nights when my days once re-volved a-round you.

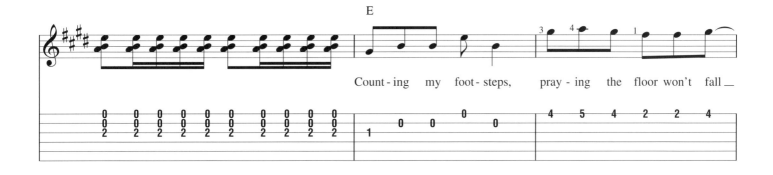

Count-ing my foot-steps, pray-ing the floor won't fall ___

___ through __ a - gain. And my moth-er ac-cused me of los-ing my mind but I

Verse

swore I was fine. _____ 2. You paint me a blue sky and go back and turn it to
may - be it's me and my blind op - ti - mism to

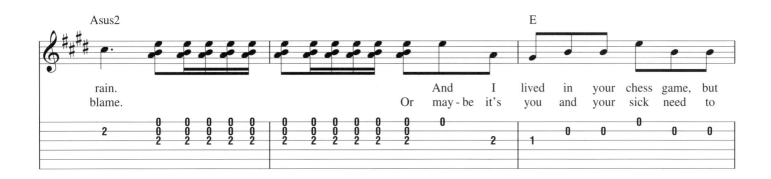

rain. And I lived in your chess game, but
blame. Or may - be it's you and your sick need to

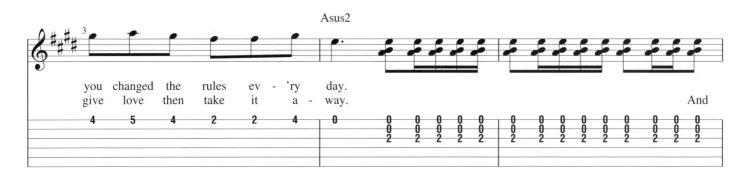

you changed the rules ev - 'ry day.
give love then take it a - way. And

Wond-'ring which ver-sion of you I might get on the phone to-
you'll add my name to your long list of trai-tors who don't un-der-

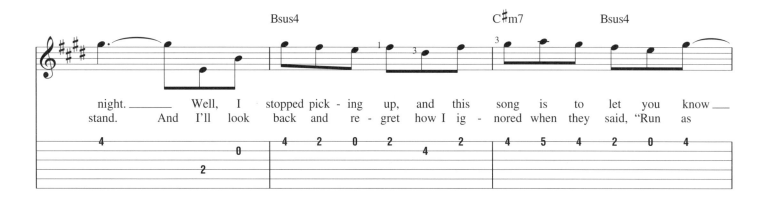

night. _____ Well, I stopped pick-ing up, and this song is to let you know ___
stand. And I'll look back and re-gret how I ig-nored when they said, "Run as

§ **Chorus**

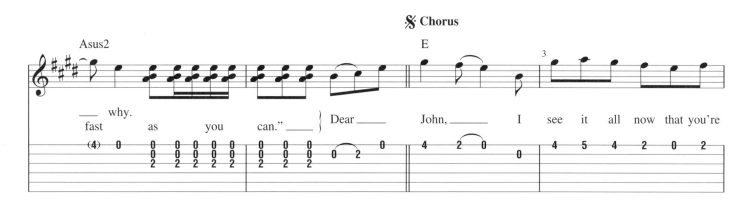

___ why.
fast as you can." ___ } Dear _____ John, _____ I see it all now that you're

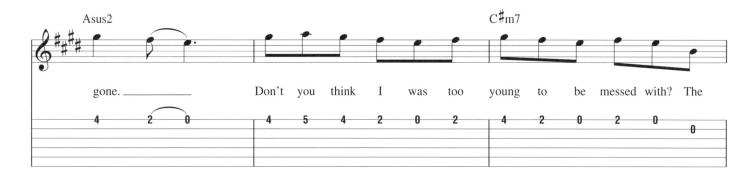

gone. _____ Don't you think I was too young to be messed with? The

To Coda ⊕ |1.   **Interlude**

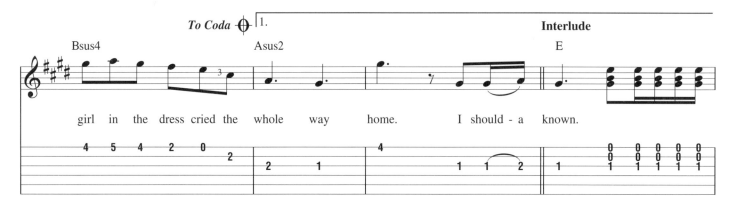

girl in the dress cried the whole way home. I should-a known.

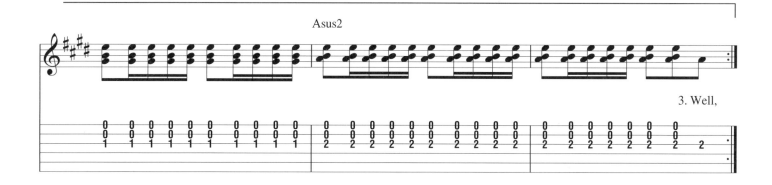

Asus2

3. Well,

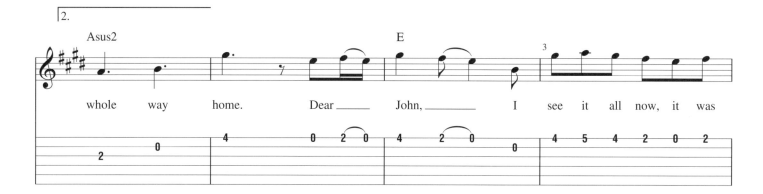

2.

Asus2   E

whole   way   home.   Dear ____ John, _____   I   see   it   all   now,   it   was

Asus2   C#m7   Bsus4

wrong. ____   Don't you think nine-teen's too young to   be played by your dark, twist-ed games when I

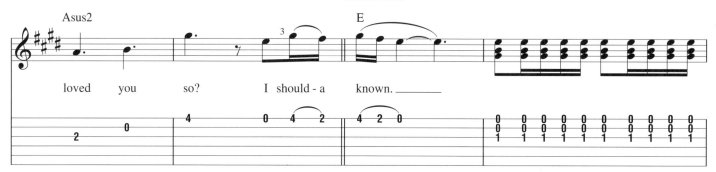

Guitar Solo

Asus2   E

loved   you   so?   I   should-a   known. _____

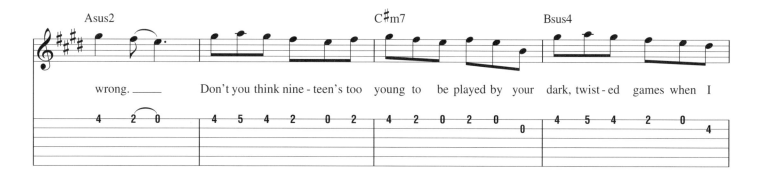

Bridge

Asus2   C#m7   Bsus4

You are an   ex-pert at   sor-ry, and keep-ing lines blur-ry.

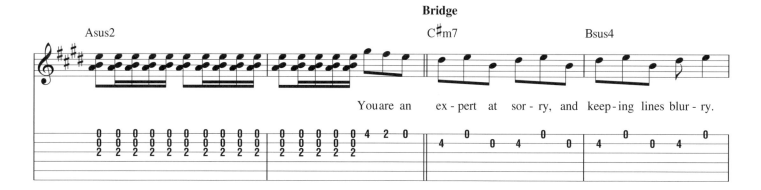

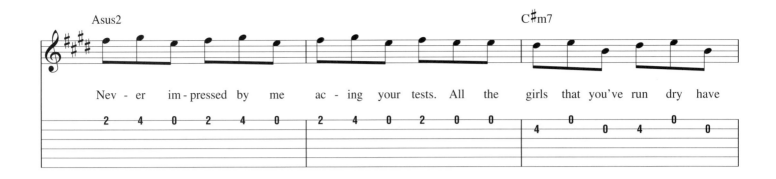

Nev - er im - pressed by me ac - ing your tests. All the girls that you've run dry have

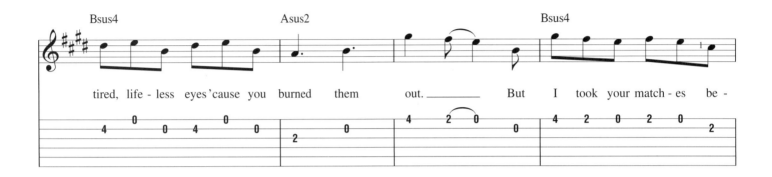

tired, life - less eyes 'cause you burned them out. _____ But I took your match - es be -

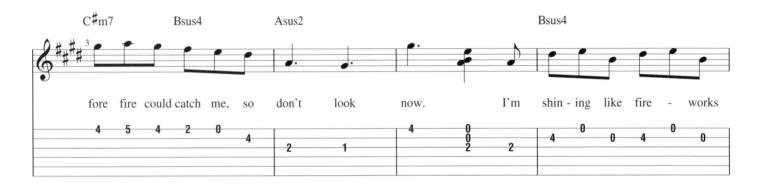

fore fire could catch me, so don't look now. I'm shin - ing like fire - works

Interlude

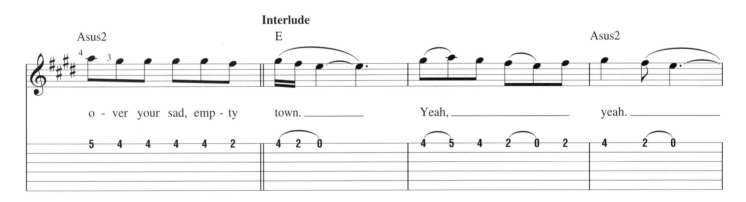

o - ver your sad, emp - ty town. _____ Yeah, _____ yeah. _____

D.S. al Coda

_____ Oh, _____ oh. _____ Dear _____

Coda

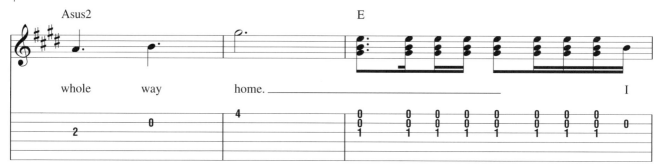

whole way home. _____ I

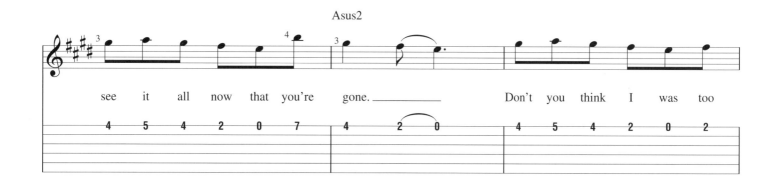

see it all now that you're gone. _____ Don't you think I was too

young to be messed with? The girl in the dress wrote you a song. You should-'ve

Outro

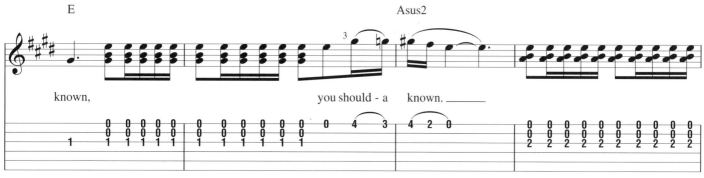

known, you should-a known. _____

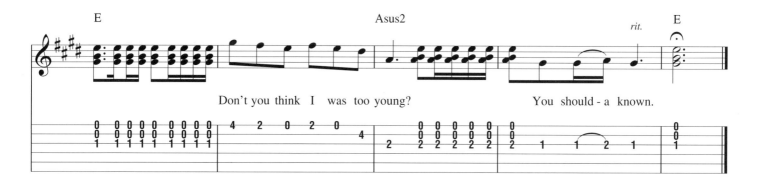

Don't you think I was too young? You should-a known.

The Story of Us

Words and Music by Taylor Swift

Strum Pattern: 1, 2
Pick Pattern: 1, 2

Intro
Moderately fast

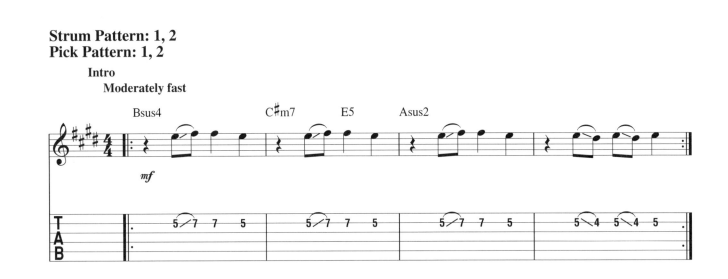

Verse

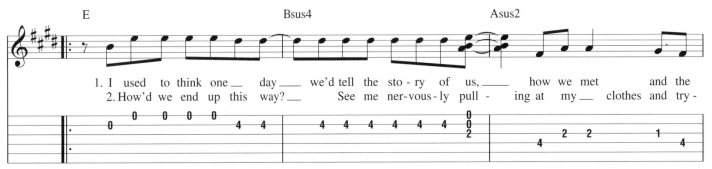

1. I used to think one ___ day ___ we'd tell the sto-ry of us, ___ how we met ___ and the
2. How'd we end up this way? ___ See me ner-vous-ly pull - ing at my ___ clothes and try-

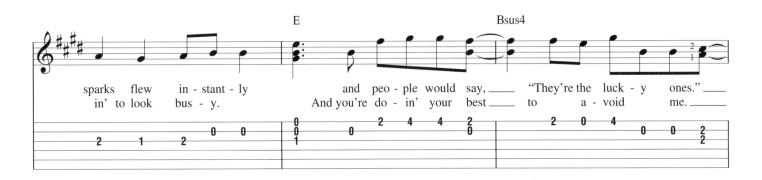

sparks flew in-stant-ly and peo-ple would say, ___ "They're the luck-y ones." ___
in' to look bus-y. And you're do-in' your best ___ to a-void me. ___

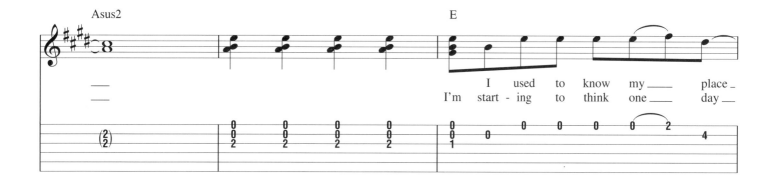

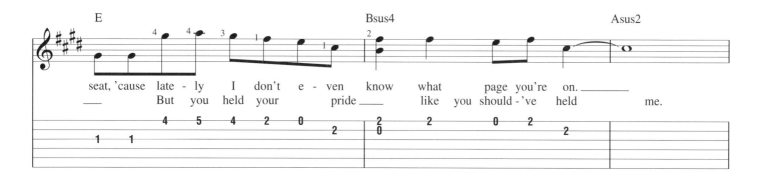

Pre-Chorus

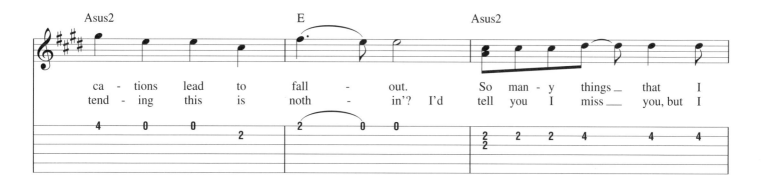

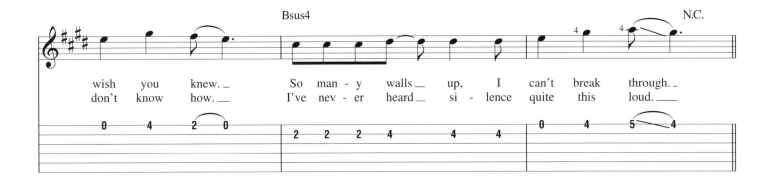

wish you knew. __ So man-y walls __ up, I can't break through. __
don't know how. __ I've nev-er heard __ si-lence quite this loud. __

 Chorus

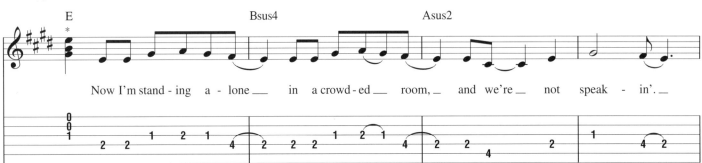

Now I'm stand-ing a-lone __ in a crowd-ed __ room, __ and we're __ not speak-in'. __

*Sung one octave higher throughout Chorus.

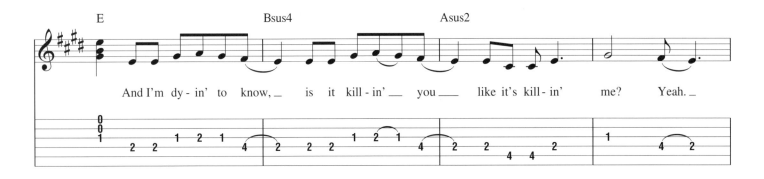

And I'm dy-in' to know, __ is it kill-in' __ you __ like it's kill-in' me? Yeah. __

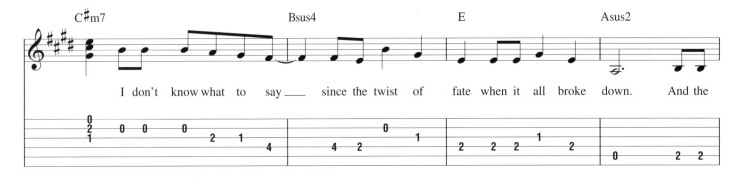

I don't know what to say __ since the twist of fate when it all broke down. And the

To Coda ⊕

|1.

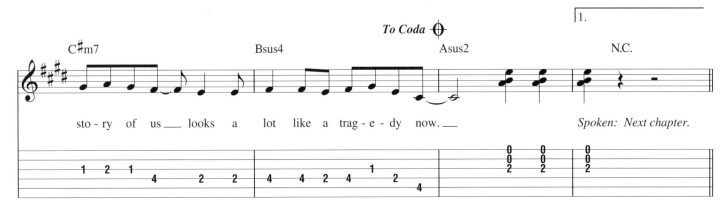

sto-ry of us __ looks a lot like a trag-e-dy now. __ *Spoken: Next chapter.*

Interlude

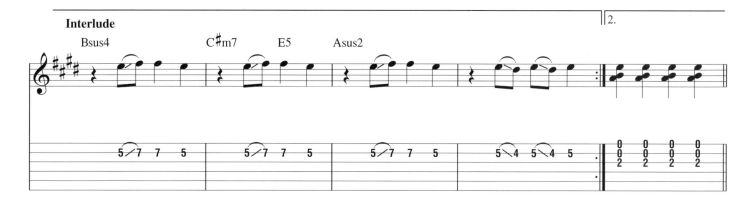

Guitar Solo

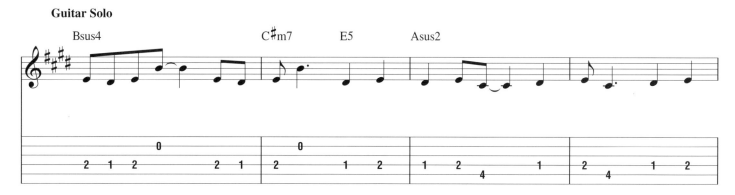

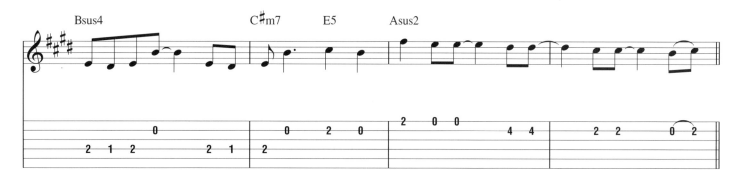

Bridge

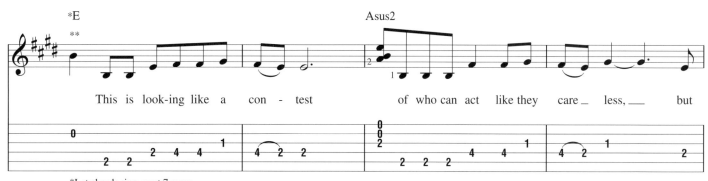

This is look-ing like a con - test of who can act like they care __ less, __ but

*Let chords ring, next 7 meas.
**Sung one octave higher till end.

I liked it bet - ter when you were on ___ my side.

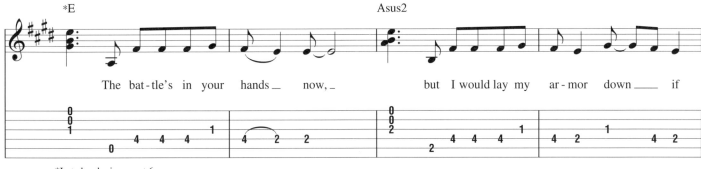

*E ... Asus2

The bat-tle's in your hands ___ now, ___ but I would lay my ar-mor down ___ if

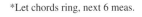
*Let chords ring, next 6 meas.

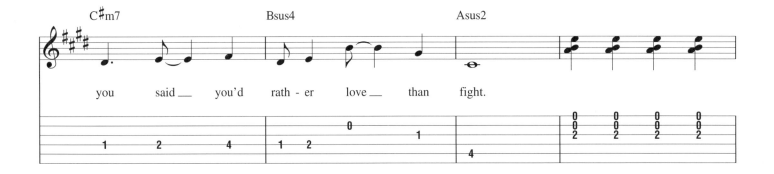

C#m7 ... Bsus4 ... Asus2

you said ___ you'd rath-er love ___ than fight.

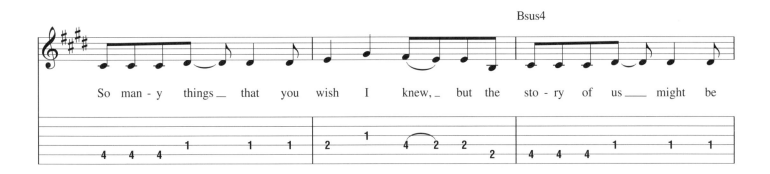

Bsus4

So man-y things ___ that you wish I knew, ___ but the sto-ry of us ___ might be

D.S. al Coda   ⊕ **Coda**

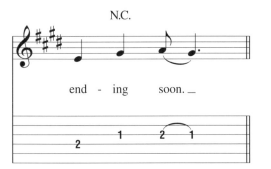

N.C.

end - ing soon. ___

Asus2

___ Now, ___ now. ___

Outro-Chorus

E ... Bsus4 ... Asus2

And we're ___ not speak - in'. ___

And I'm dy-in' to know, ___ is it kill-in' ___ you ___ like it's kill-in'

me? _____ Yeah. I don't know what to say ___ since the twist of

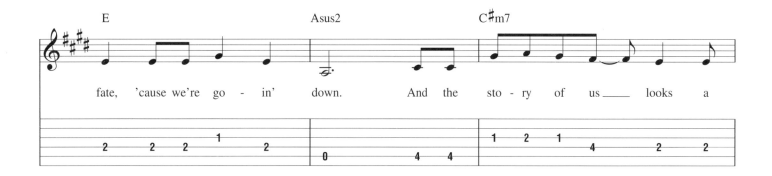

fate, 'cause we're go - in' down. And the sto - ry of us ___ looks a

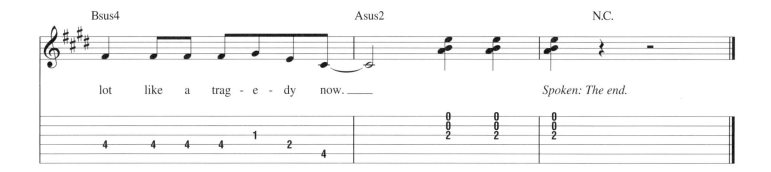

lot like a trag - e - dy now. ___ *Spoken: The end.*

Never Grow Up

Words and Music by Taylor Swift

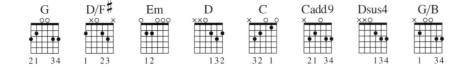

*Capo VII

Strum Pattern: 3
Pick Pattern: 3

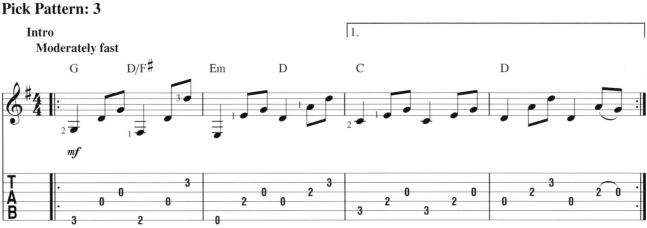

*Optional: To match recording, place capo at 7th fret.

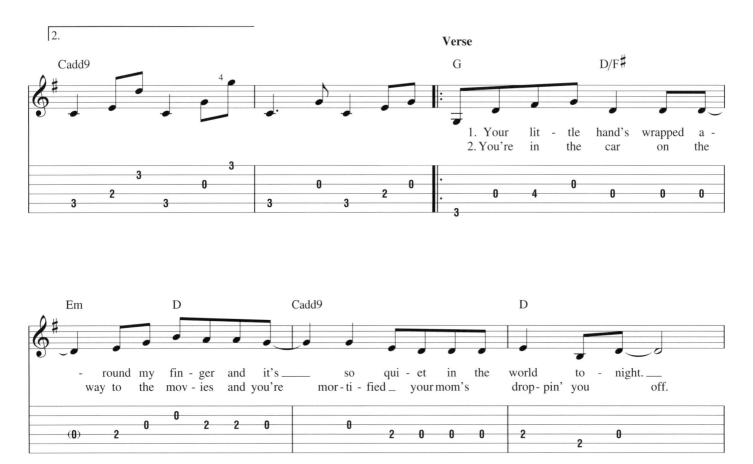

1. Your lit-tle hand's wrapped a-round my fin-ger and it's ___ so qui-et in the world to-night. ___
2. You're in the car on the way to the mov-ies and you're mor-ti-fied ___ your mom's drop-pin' you off.

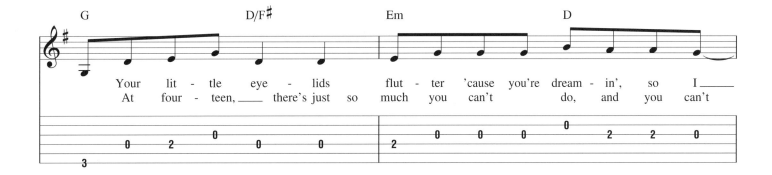

Your lit - tle eye - lids flut - ter 'cause you're dream - in', so I _____
At four - teen, _____ there's just so much you can't do, and you can't

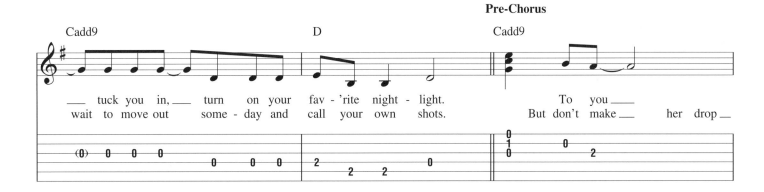

Pre-Chorus

_____ tuck you in, _____ turn on your fav - 'rite night - light. To you _____
wait to move out some - day and call your own shots. But don't make _____ her drop _____

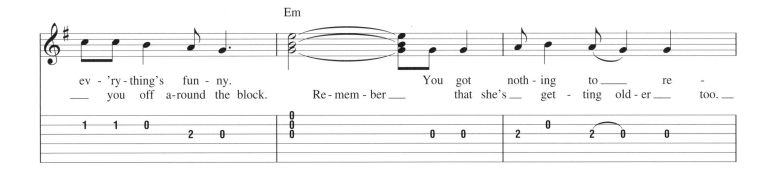

ev - 'ry - thing's fun - ny. You got noth - ing to _____ re -
_____ you off a - round the block. Re - mem - ber _____ that she's _____ get - ting old - er _____ too. _____

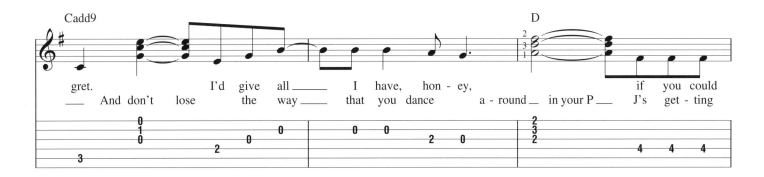

gret. I'd give all _____ I have, hon - ey, if you could
_____ And don't lose the way _____ that you dance a - round _____ in your P _____ J's get - ting

Chorus

stay like that. Oo, dar - lin', don't you ev - er grow up. Don't you
read - y for school.

43

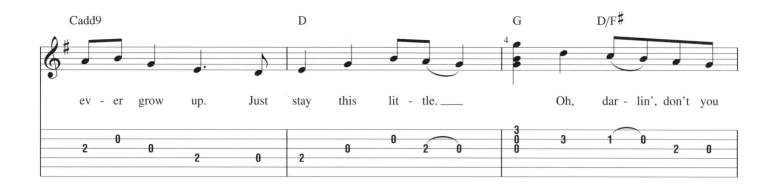

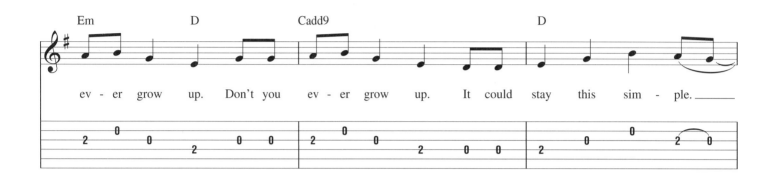

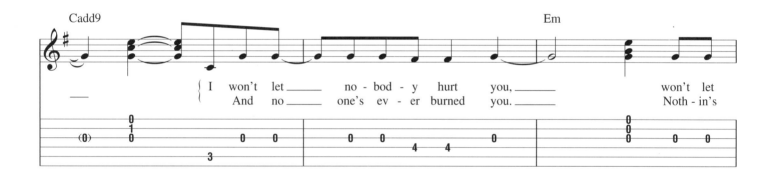

Interlude

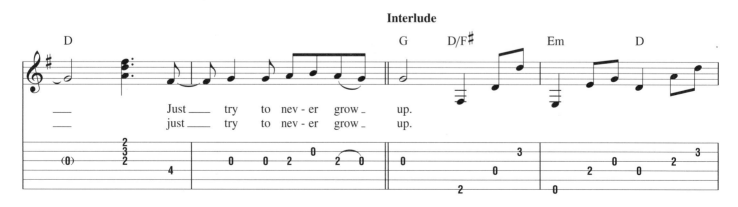

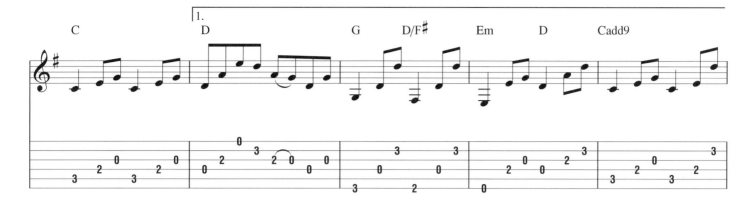

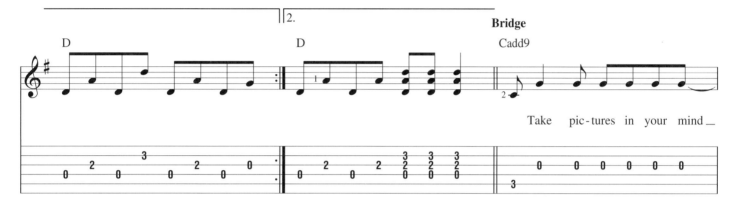

Take pic - tures in your mind ___

___ of your child - hood room. _____ Mem - o - rize what it sound -

- ed like when your dad ___ gets home. Re - mem - ber the foot - steps, re - mem - ber the words ___

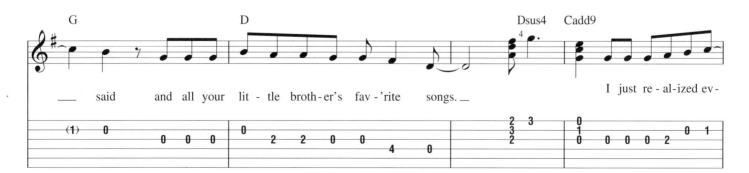

___ said and all your lit - tle broth - er's fav - 'rite songs. ___ I just re - al - ized ev -

-'ry - thing I have is some - day gon - na be gone. 3. So, here I am in my __

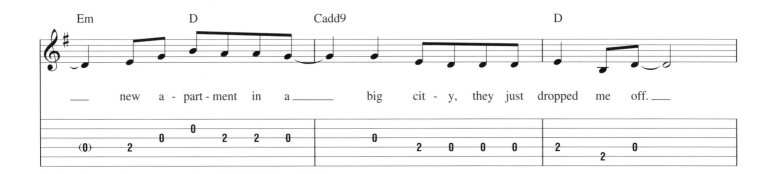

__ new a - part - ment in a _____ big cit - y, they just dropped me off. __

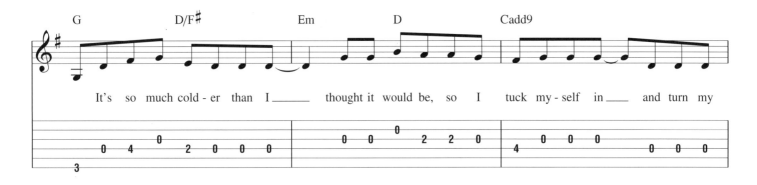

It's so much cold - er than I _____ thought it would be, so I tuck my - self in ___ and turn my

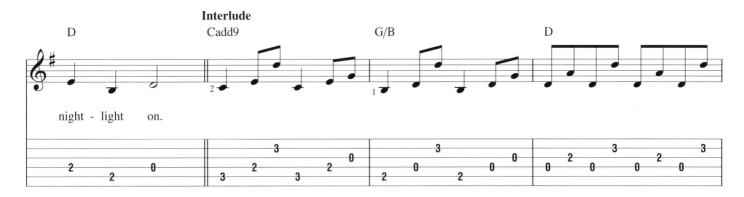

night - light on.

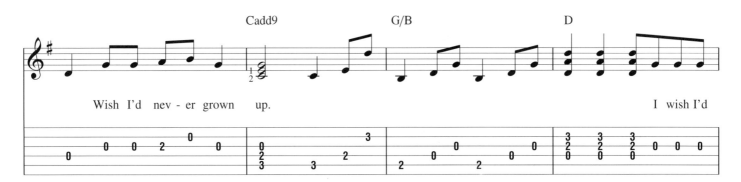

Wish I'd nev - er grown up. I wish I'd

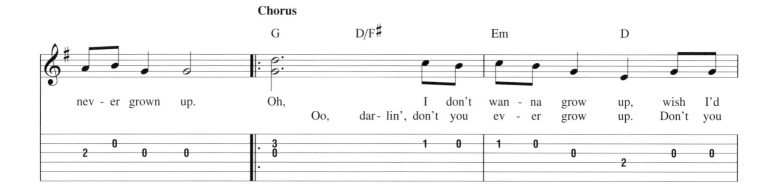

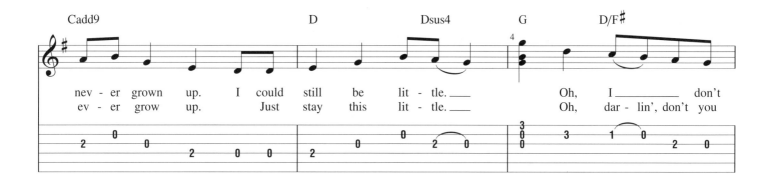

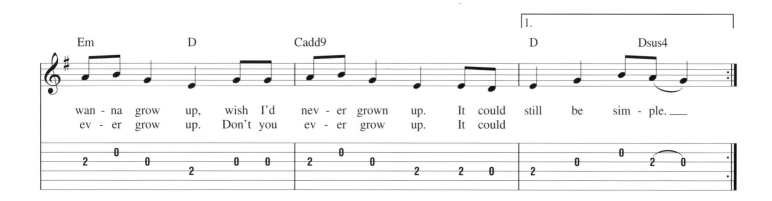

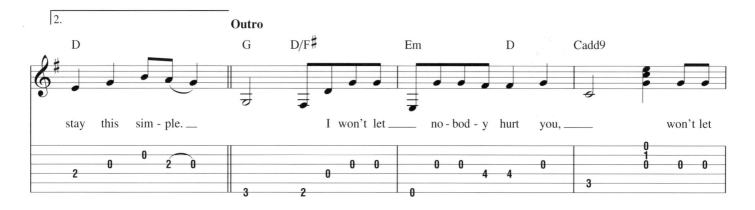

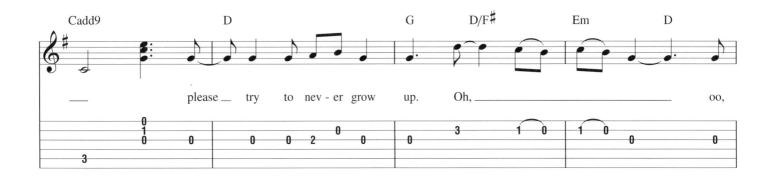

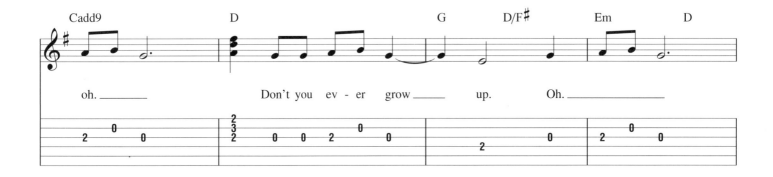

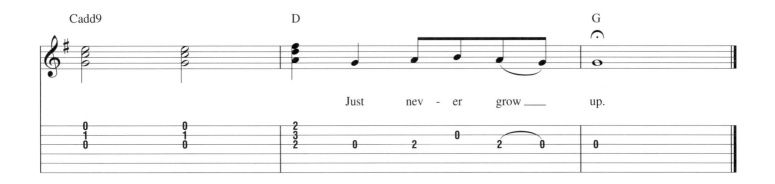

Enchanted

Words and Music by Taylor Swift

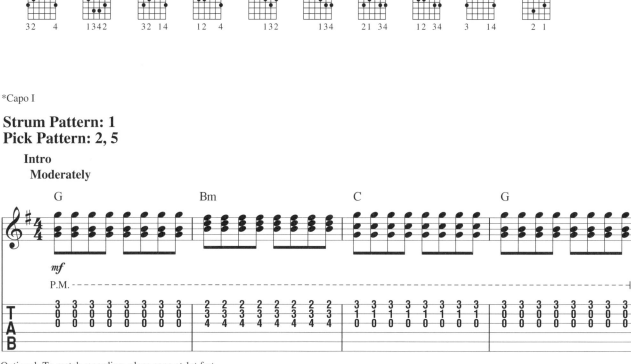

*Capo I

Strum Pattern: 1
Pick Pattern: 2, 5

Intro
Moderately

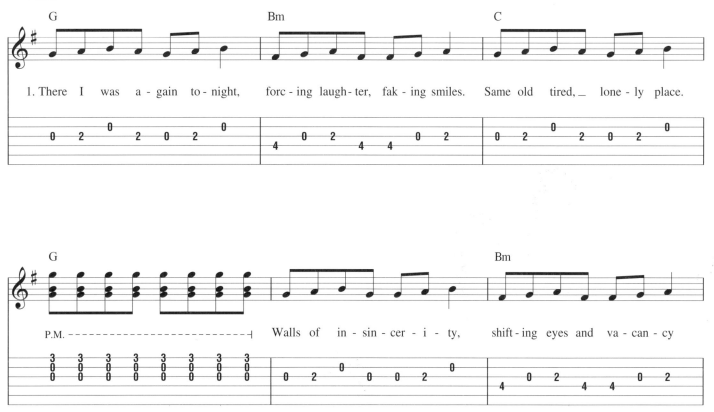

*Optional: To match recording, place capo at 1st fret.

Verse

1. There I was a-gain to-night, forc-ing laugh-ter, fak-ing smiles. Same old tired,__ lone-ly place.

Walls of in-sin-cer-i-ty, shift-ing eyes and va-can-cy

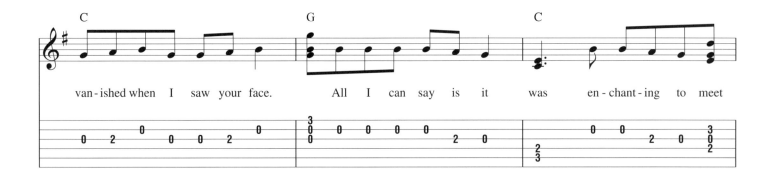

van-ished when I saw your face. All I can say is it was en-chant-ing to meet

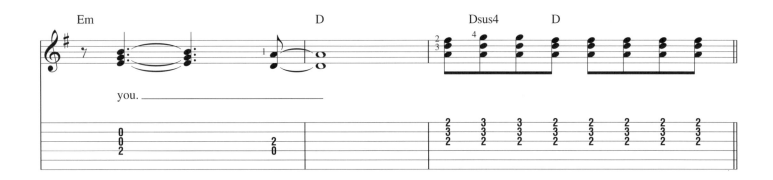

you.

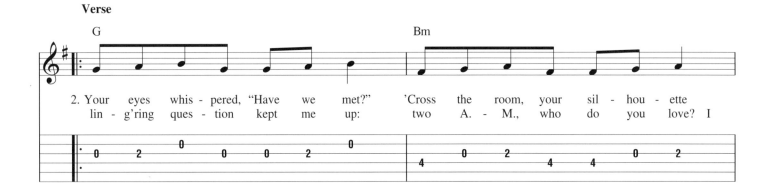

Verse

2. Your eyes whis-pered, "Have we met?" 'Cross the room, your sil-hou-ette
lin-g'ring ques-tion kept me up: two A. - M., who do you love? I

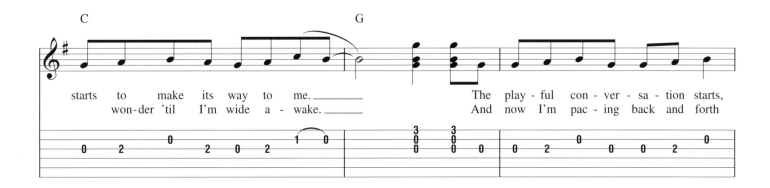

starts to make its way to me._____ The play-ful con-ver-sa-tion starts,
won-der 'til I'm wide a-wake._____ And now I'm pac-ing back and forth

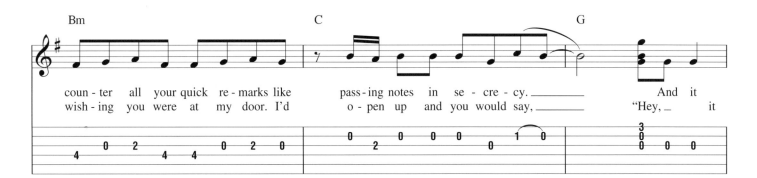

coun - ter all your quick re-marks like pass-ing notes in se-cre-cy._____ And it
wish - ing you were at my door. I'd o-pen up and you would say,_____ "Hey,__ it

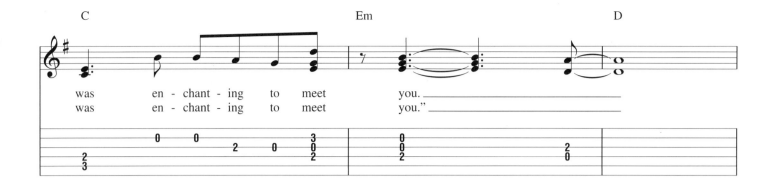

was en - chant - ing to meet you. _____
was en - chant - ing to meet you." _____

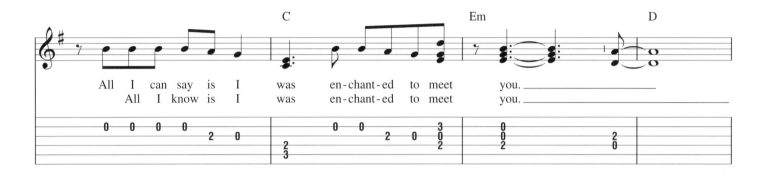

All I can say is I was en - chant - ed to meet you. _____
All I know is I was en - chant - ed to meet you. _____

𝄋 **Chorus**

This night is spark - lin', don't you let it

*Sung one octave higher throughout Chorus.

go. I'm won - der - struck, blush-ing all the way home. __ I'll spend for - ev - er won - d'rin' if you

1.

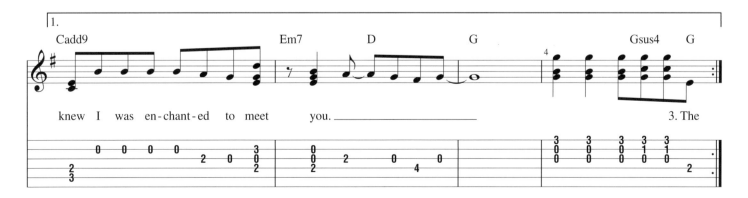

knew I was en - chant - ed to meet you. _____ 3. The

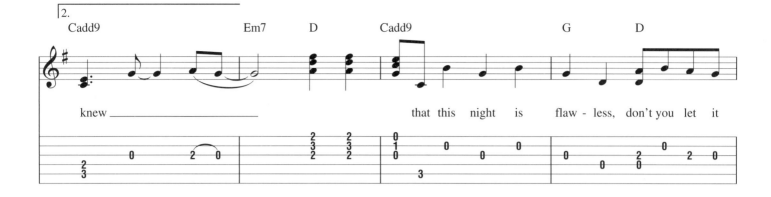

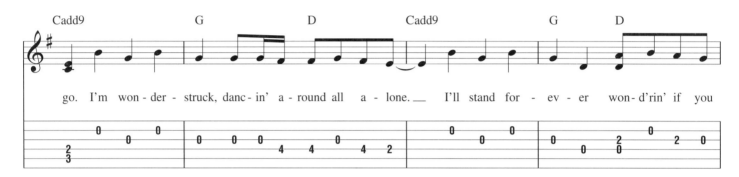

To Coda ⊕

Guitar Solo

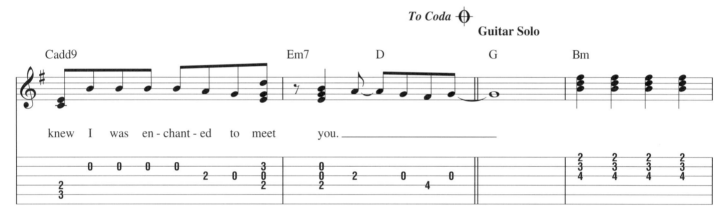

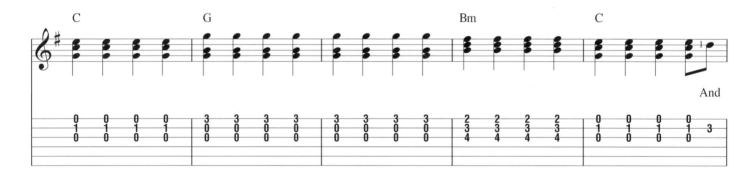

Bridge

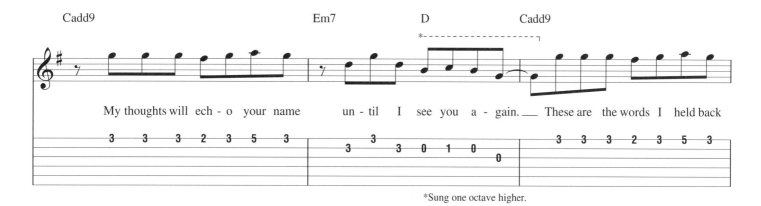

My thoughts will ech - o your name   un - til I see you a - gain. ___ These are the words I held back

*Sung one octave higher.

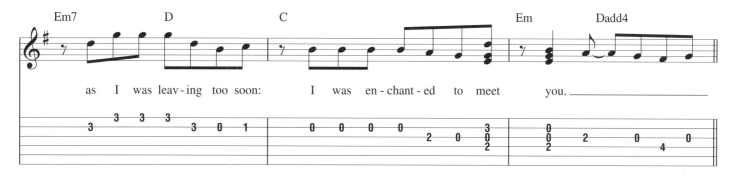

as   I   was leav - ing too soon: I   was en - chant - ed   to   meet   you. _____

Interlude
w/ Lead Voc. ad lib.

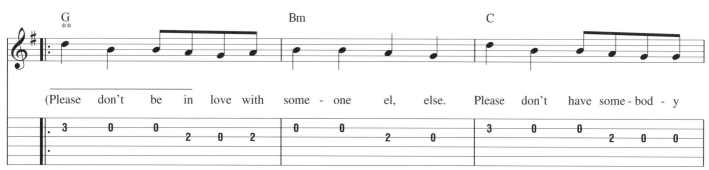

(Please   don't   be   in   love with   some - one   el, else.   Please   don't   have some - bod - y

**2nd time, sung one octave higher.

2nd time, D.S. al Coda
(take 2nd ending)

⊕ **Coda**
Outro

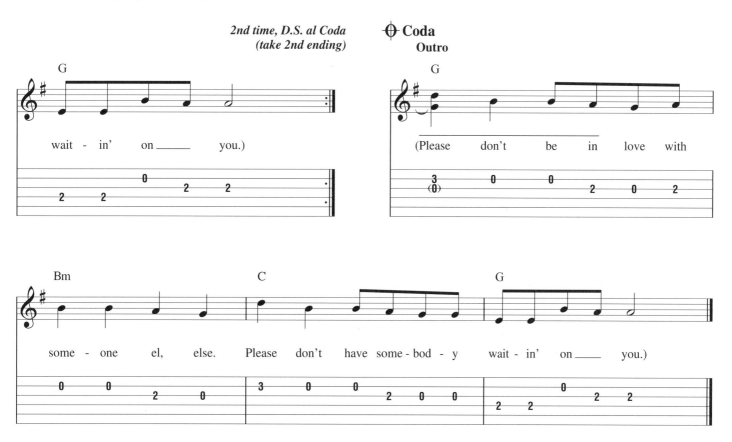

wait - in'   on ___   you.)

(Please   don't   be   in   love with

some - one   el, else.   Please   don't   have some - bod - y   wait - in'   on ___   you.)

Innocent

Words and Music by Taylor Swift

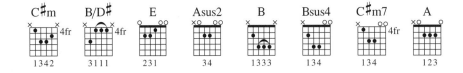

Strum Pattern: 1, 3
Pick Pattern: 1, 3

Intro
Slowly, in 2

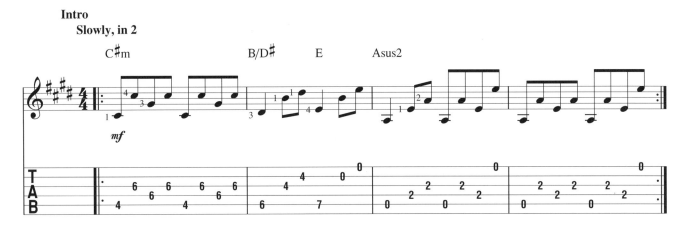

Verse

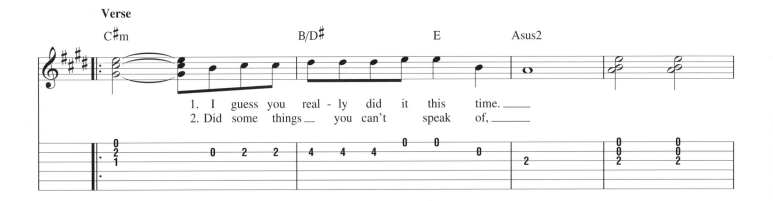

1. I guess you real - ly did it this time. _____
2. Did some things _____ you can't speak of, _____

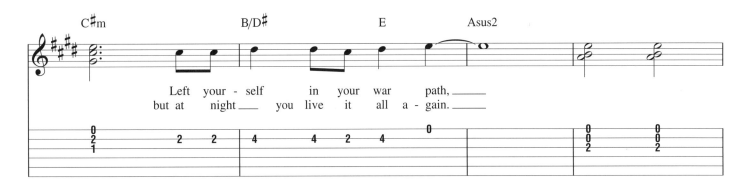

Left your - self in your war path, _____
but at night _____ you live it all a - gain. _____

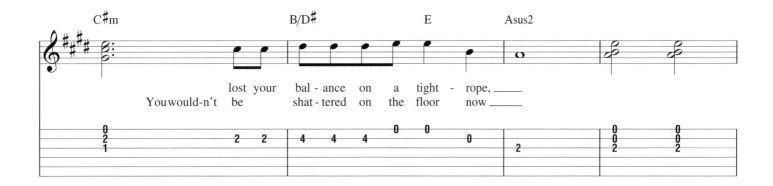

lost your bal-ance on a tight-rope,____
You would-n't be shat-tered on the floor now ____

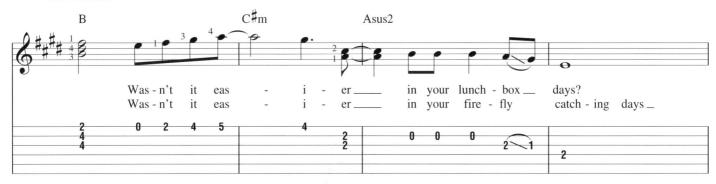

lost your mind try'n' to get it back. ____
if on-ly you had seen what you know now ____ then.

Pre-Chorus

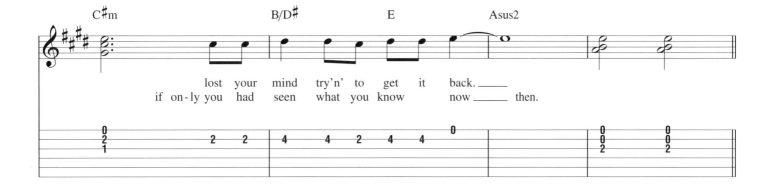

Was-n't it eas - i - er ____ in your lunch - box __ days?
Was-n't it eas - i - er ____ in your fire - fly catch - ing days __

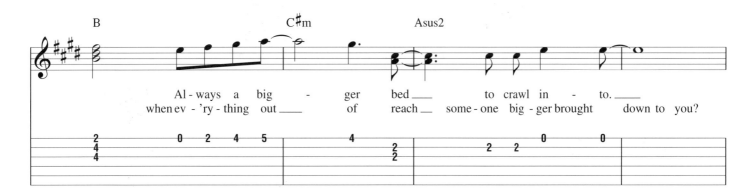

Al - ways a big - ger bed ____ to crawl in - to. ____
when ev - 'ry - thing out ____ of reach __ some - one big - ger brought down to you?

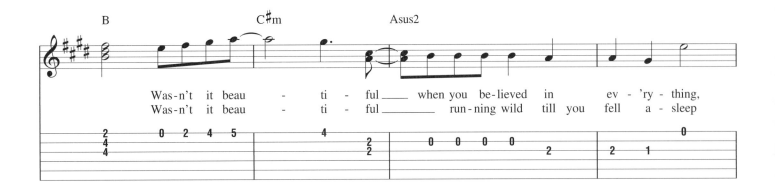

Was-n't it beau - ti - ful _____ when you be-lieved in ev - 'ry - thing,
Was-n't it beau - ti - ful _____ run-ning wild till you fell a - sleep

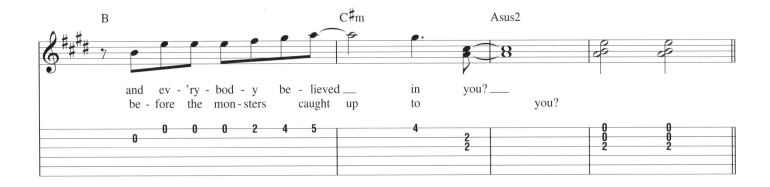

and ev - 'ry - bod - y be - lieved ___ in you? ___
be - fore the mon-sters caught up to you?

§ Chorus

It's al - right, just ___ wait and see. Your _____ string of lights are still ___ bright to me. Oh,

*Sung one octave higher throughout Chorus.

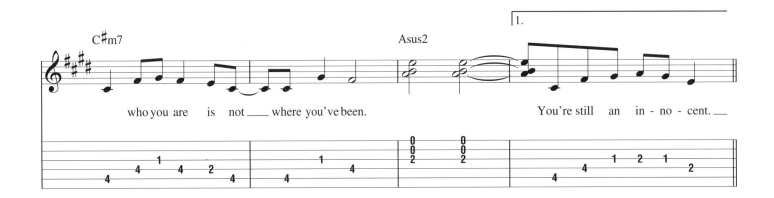

who you are is not ___ where you've been.

1.

You're still an in - no - cent. ___

Interlude

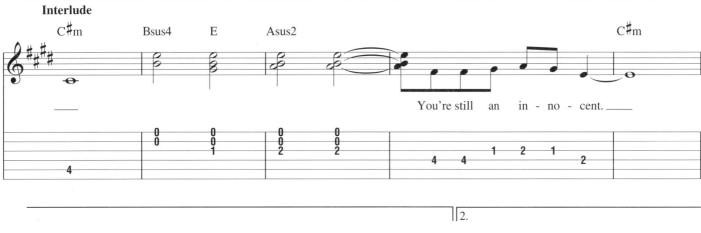

You're still an in - no - cent. ___

You're still an in - no - cent.

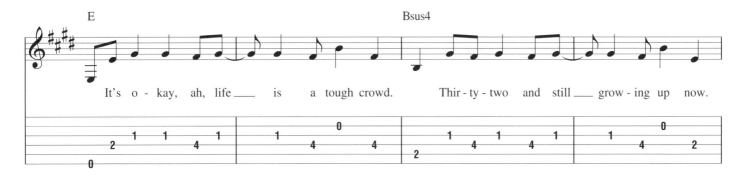

It's o - kay, ah, life ___ is a tough crowd. Thir - ty - two and still ___ grow - ing up now.

To Coda ⊕

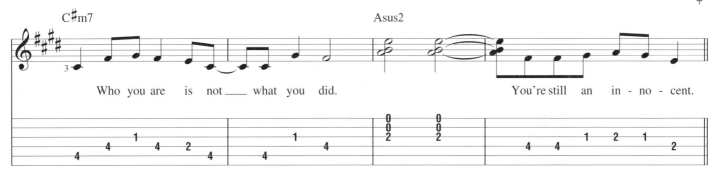

Who you are is not ___ what you did. You're still an in - no - cent.

Interlude

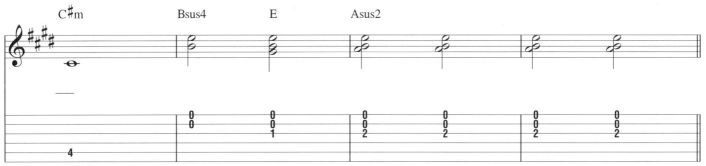

Bridge

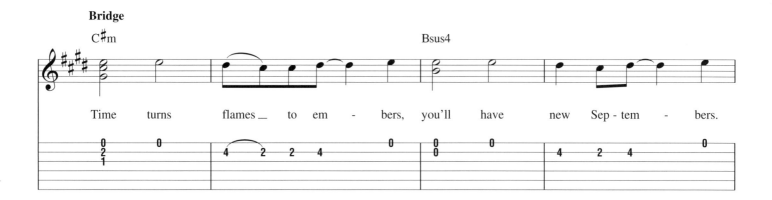

Time turns flames to em - bers, you'll have new Sep - tem - bers.

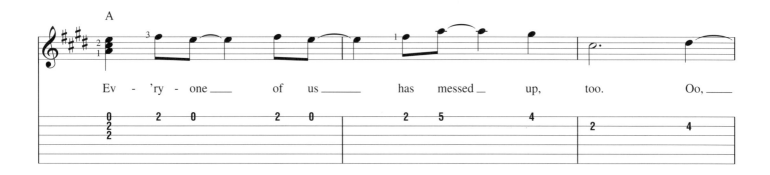

Ev - 'ry - one of us has messed up, too. Oo,

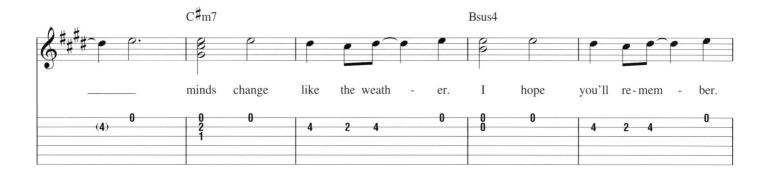

minds change like the weath - er. I hope you'll re - mem - ber.

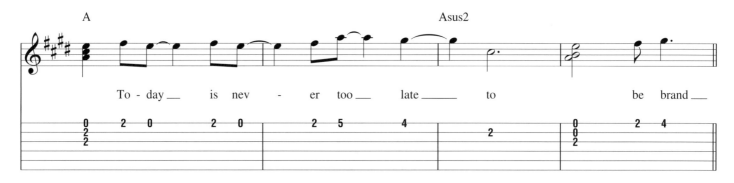

To - day is nev - er too late to be brand

Guitar Solo

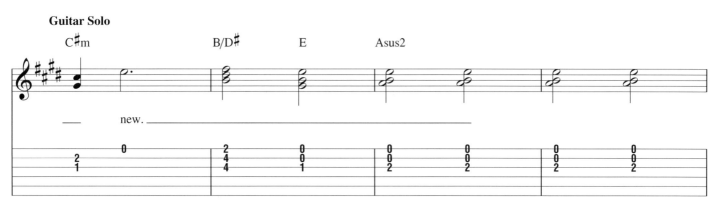

new.

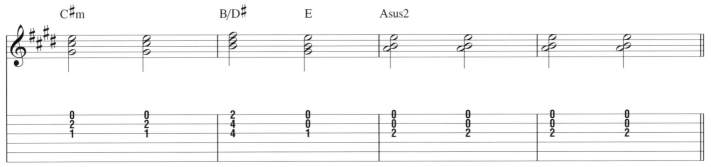

 Coda

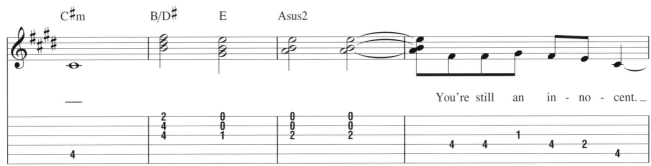

You're still an in - no - cent.

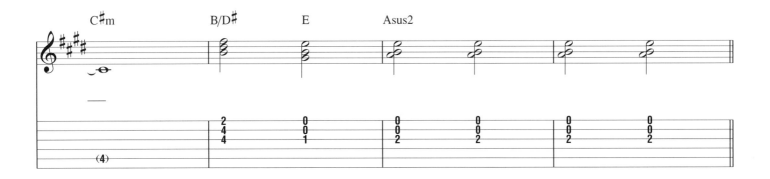

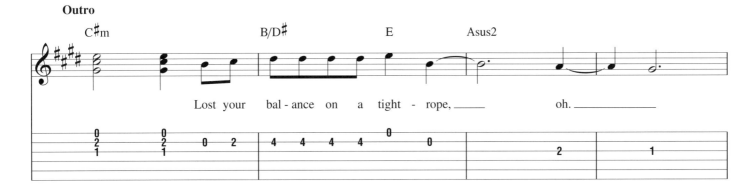

Lost your bal - ance on a tight - rope, _____ oh. _____

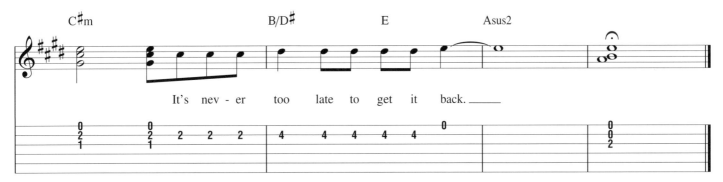

It's nev - er too late to get it back. _____

Haunted

Words and Music by Taylor Swift

*Tune down 1 step:
(low to high) D-G-C-F-A-D

Strum Pattern: 1
Pick Pattern: 5

*Optional: To match recording, tune down 1 step.

**Strings arr. for gtr.

***Sung one octave higher throughout.

1. You and I _____ walk a fra-gile line. _ I have known _ it all _ this time, but I nev-er thought I'd live to see _ it break.
2. Stood there and watched you walk a-way _____ from ev-'ry-thing we had, but I still mean ev-'ry word _ I said to you. It's get-ting dark and it's He will try _ to take a-

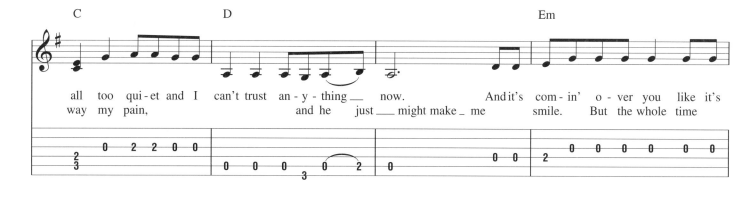

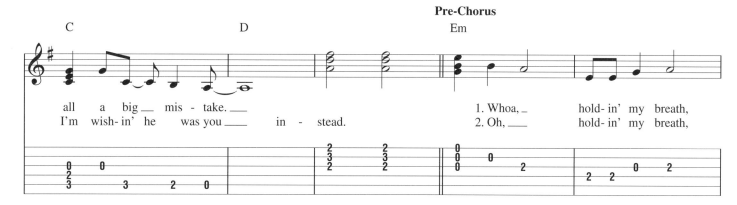

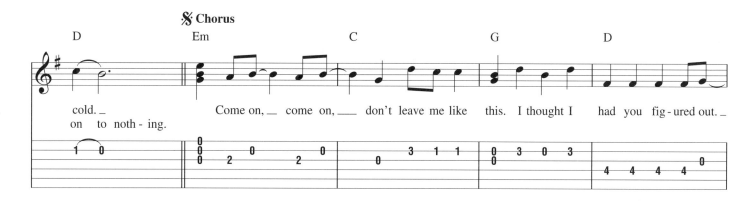

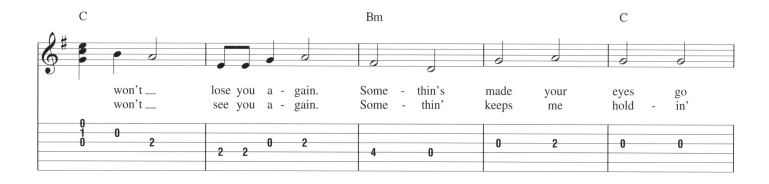

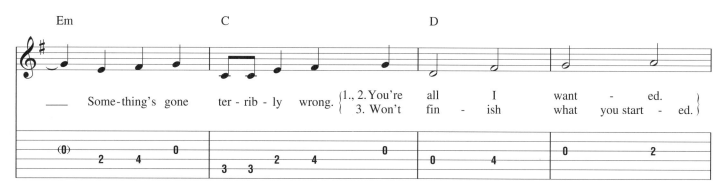

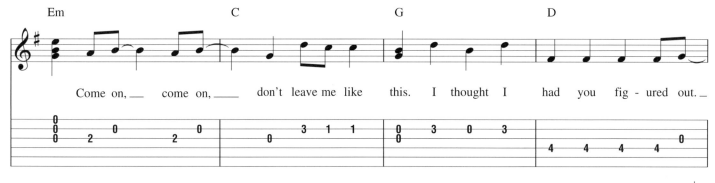

Come on, __ come on, __ don't leave me like this. I thought I had you fig - ured out. __

To Coda ⊕

__ Can't breathe when - ev - er you're gone. Can't turn back now. I'm haunt - ed.

Interlude

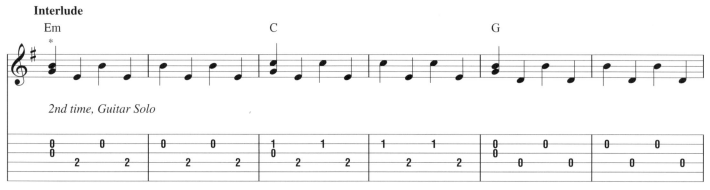

2nd time, Guitar Solo

*Strings arr. for guitar.

Bridge

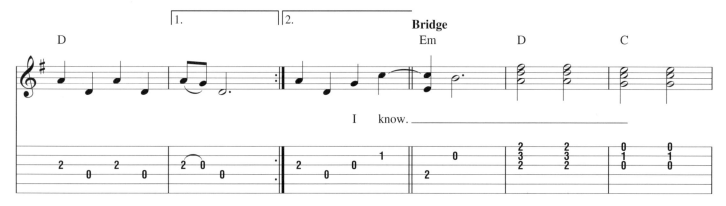

1. ‖ 2.

I know. __

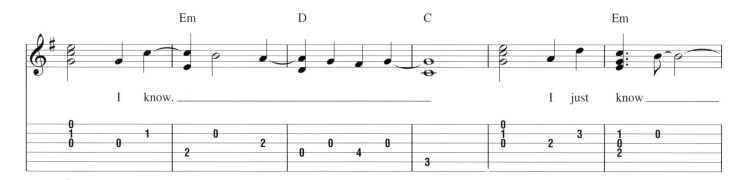

I know. __   I just know __

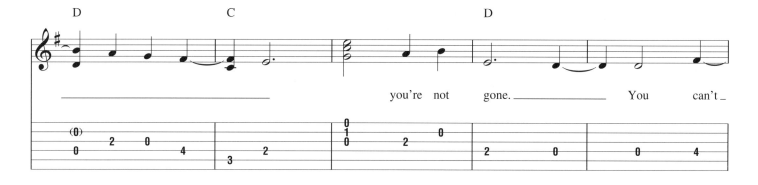

you're not gone. _____ You can't __

⊕ Coda

D.S. al Coda

Interlude

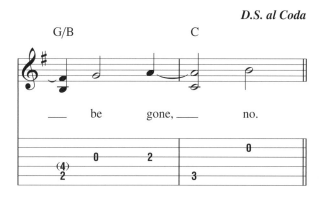

__ be gone, ___ no.

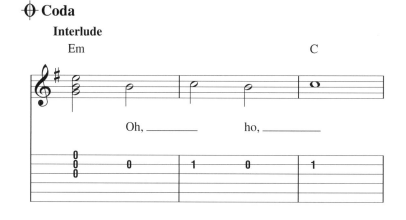

Oh, _____ ho, _____

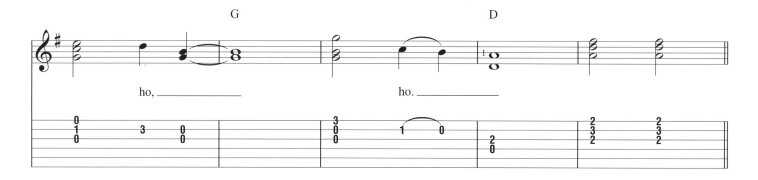

ho, _____ ho. _____

Outro

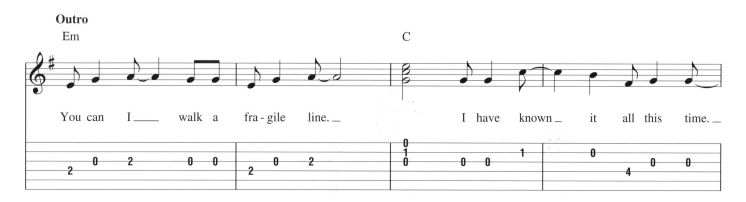

You can I __ walk a fra-gile line. _ I have known __ it all this time. __

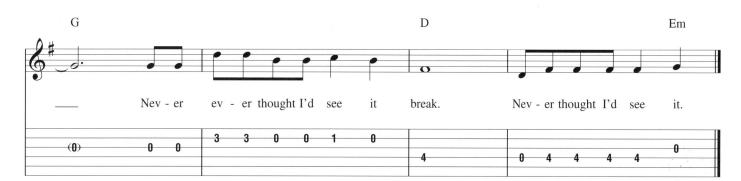

__ Nev-er ev-er thought I'd see it break. Nev-er thought I'd see it.

Last Kiss

Words and Music by Taylor Swift

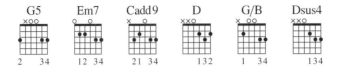

*Capo III

Strum Pattern: 8
Pick Pattern: 8

Intro
Slowly

*Optional: To match recording, place capo at 3rd fret.

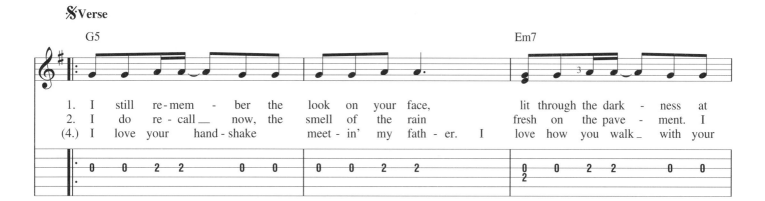

Verse

G5   Em7

1. I still re-mem-ber the look on your face, lit through the dark-ness at
2. I do re-call___ now, the smell of the rain fresh on the pave-ment. I
(4.) I love your hand-shake meet-in' my fath-er. I love how you walk___ with your

Cadd9

one-fif-ty-eight.___ The words that you whis-pered for
ran off the plane.___ That Ju-ly ninth,___ the
hands in your pock-ets, how'd you kiss me when I_____ was in the

1.

D

just us to know.___ You told me you loved___ me, so why did you go___
beat of your heart,___ it jumps through your shirt.___ I can
mid-dle of say-in' some-thin'. There's not a day I don't miss those

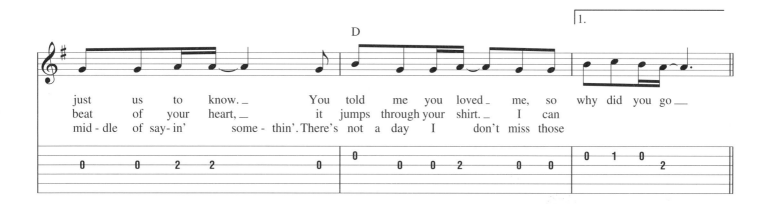

Interlude

G5   Em7

a - way? ___

65

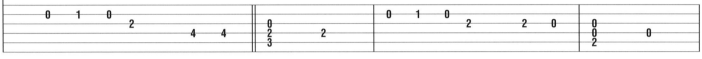

Pre-Chorus

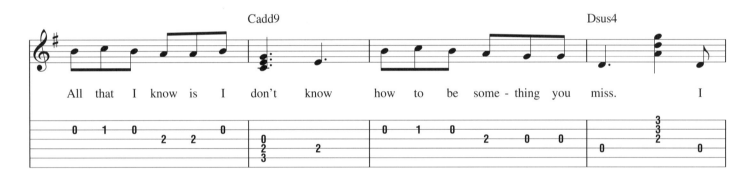

still feel your arms. _ But now
rude in - ter - rup - tions. And } I'll go sit on the floor _ wear - in' your clothes.

All that I know is I don't know how to be some - thing you miss. I

Chorus

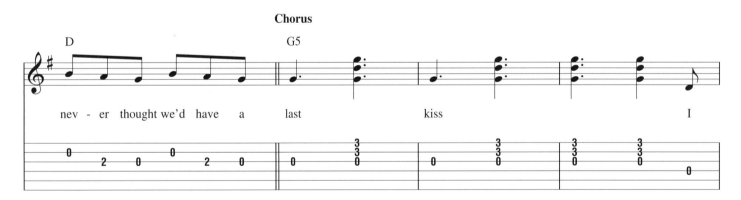

nev - er thought we'd have a last kiss I

nev - er im - ag - ined we'd end like this. _

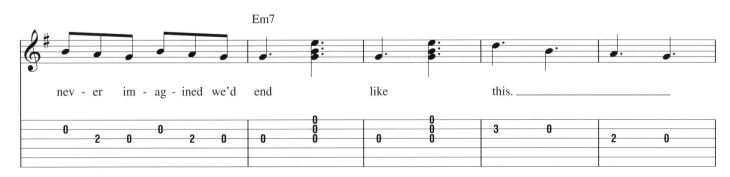

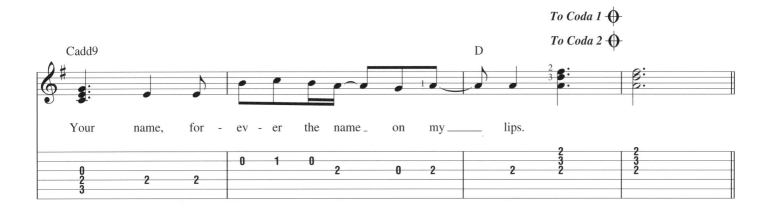

Cadd9   D

Your name, for - ev - er the name __ on my _____ lips.

Verse

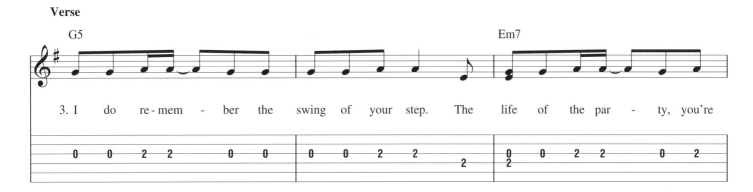

G5   Em7

3. I do re - mem - ber the swing of your step. The life of the par - ty, you're

Cadd9

show - in' off a - gain. And I roll my eyes __ and then you pull me in. __ I'm

D.S. al Coda I
(take 2nd ending)   ⊕ **Coda 1**

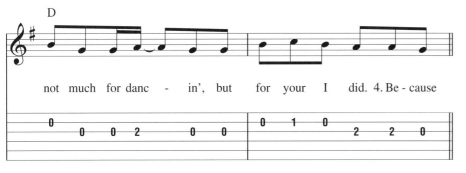

D

not much for danc - in', but for your I did. 4. Be - cause

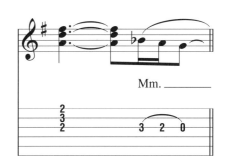

Mm. _____

Interlude   **Bridge**

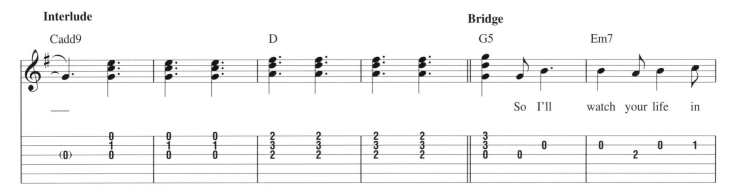

Cadd9   D   G5   Em7

___ So I'll watch your life in

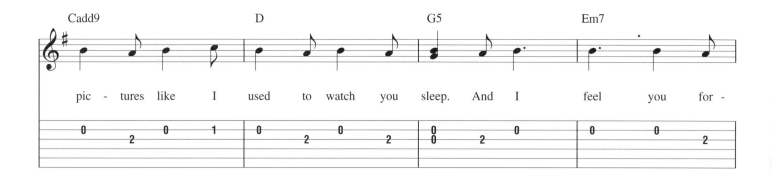

pic - tures like I used to watch you sleep. And I feel you for -

get me like I used to feel you breathe. And I'll keep — up — with our

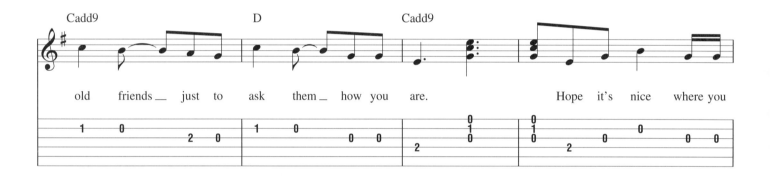

old friends — just to ask them — how you are. Hope it's nice where you

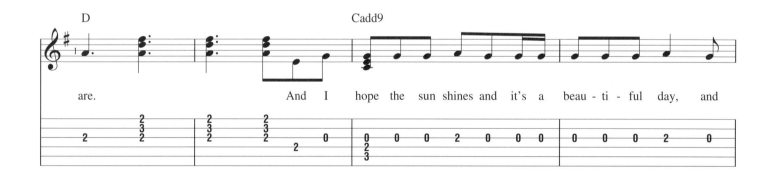

are. And I hope the sun shines and it's a beau - ti - ful day, and

some-thing re - minds — you, you wish you had stayed. You can plan for a change — in the

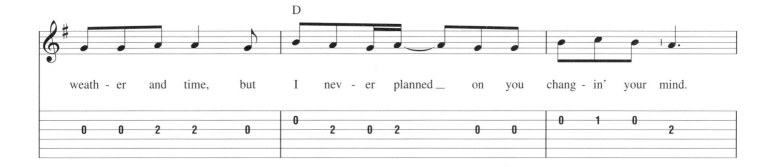

weath - er and time, but I nev - er planned ___ on you chang - in' your mind.

D.S.S. al Coda 2
(take 2nd ending)

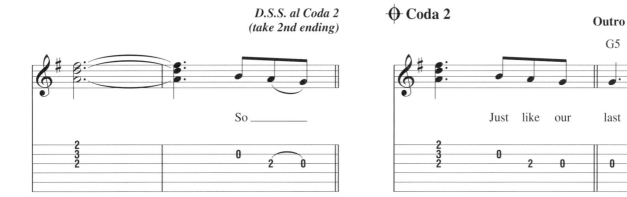

So ___

✛ **Coda 2**

Outro

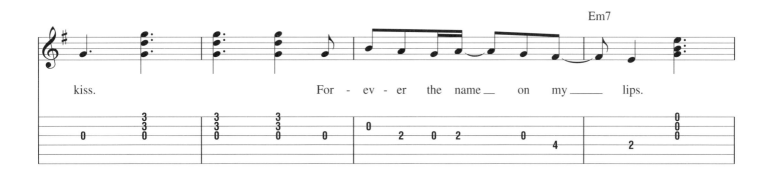

Just like our last

kiss. For - ev - er the name ___ on my ___ lips.

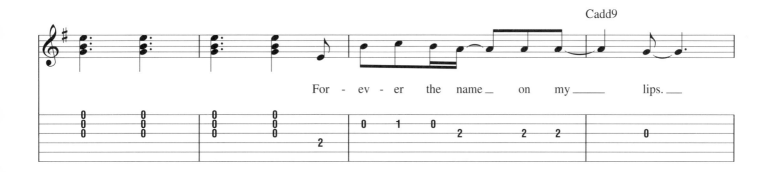

For - ev - er the name ___ on my ___ lips. ___

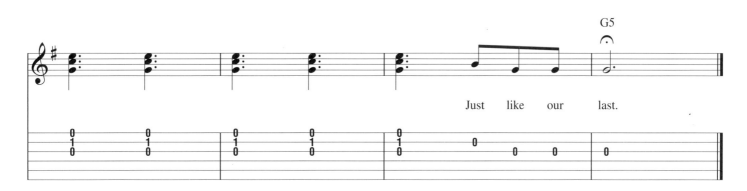

Just like our last.

Long Live

Words and Music by Taylor Swift

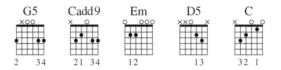

Strum Pattern: 1, 6
Pick Pattern: 4

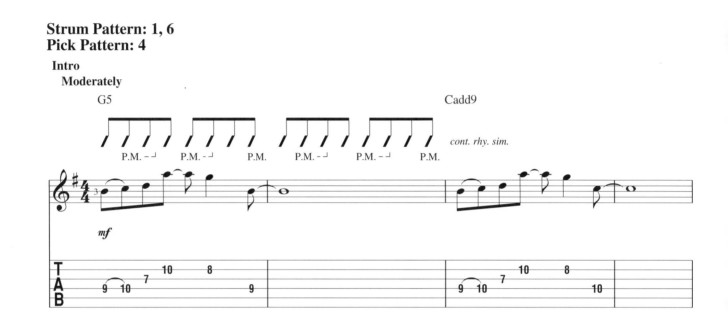

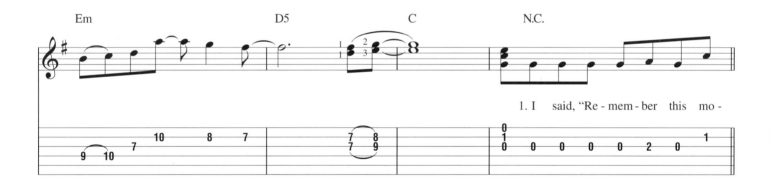

1. I said, "Re‑mem‑ber this mo‑

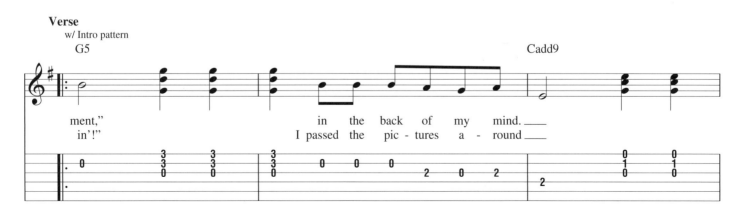

ment," in the back of my mind. ___
in'!" I passed the pic‑tures a‑round ___

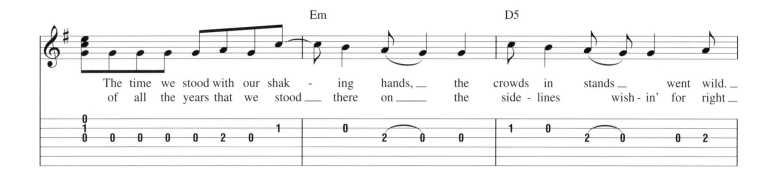

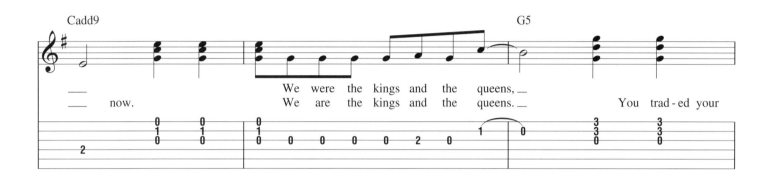

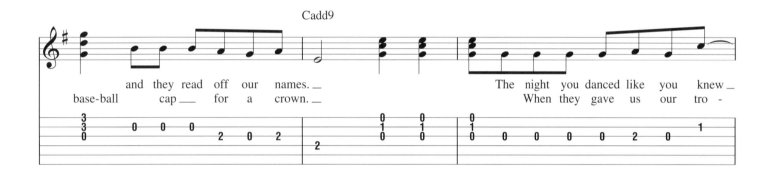

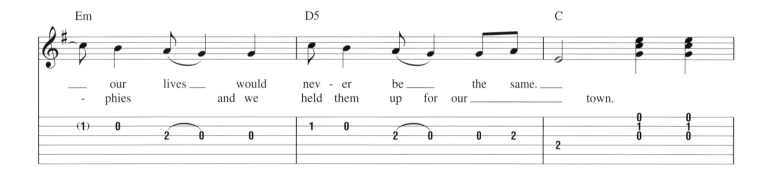

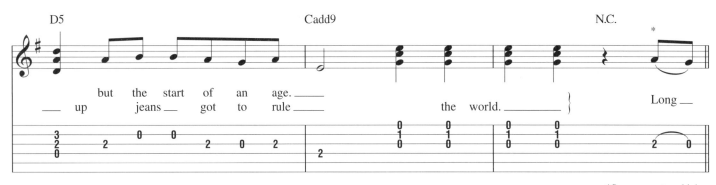

*Sung one octave higher
throughout Chorus.

𝄋 Chorus

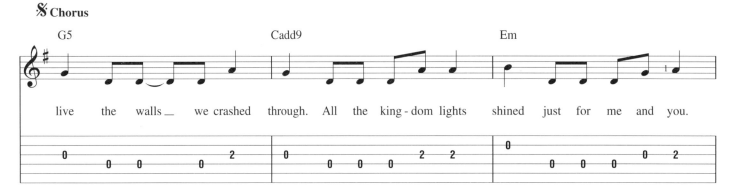

**Let chord ring.

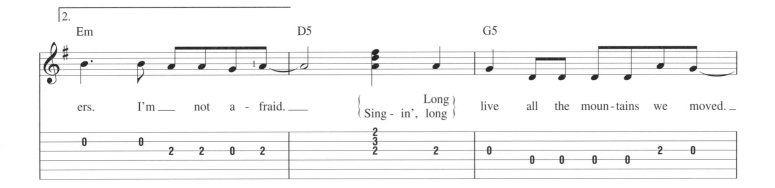

ers. I'm ___ not a-fraid. ___ {Sing-in', Long } live all the moun-tains we moved. __ {long }

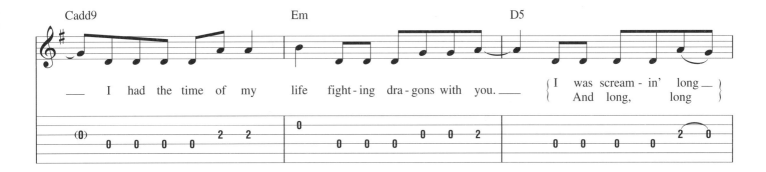

__ I had the time of my life fight-ing dra-gons with you. __ {I was scream-in' long __ } {And long, long }

To Coda ⊕

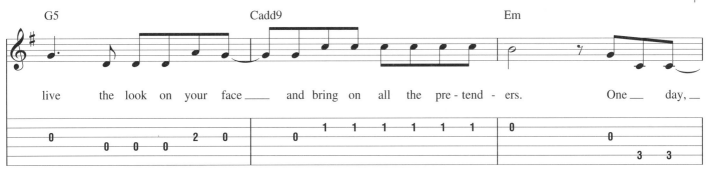

live the look on your face __ and bring on all the pre-tend-ers. One __ day, __

Bridge

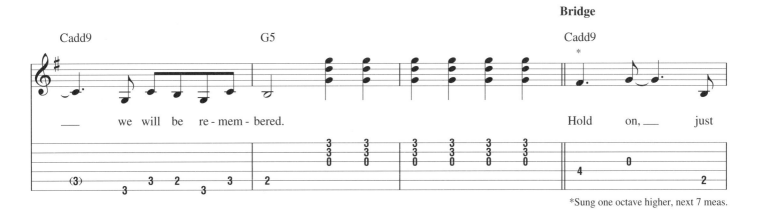

__ we will be re-mem-bered. Hold on, __ just

*Sung one octave higher, next 7 meas.

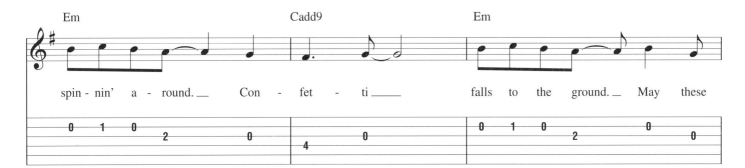

spin-nin' a-round. __ Con-fet-ti __ falls to the ground. __ May these

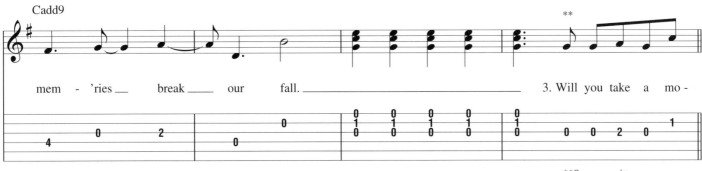

mem - 'ries___ break ___ our fall. _____ 3. Will you take a mo-

**Sung as written.

Verse
w/ Intro pattern

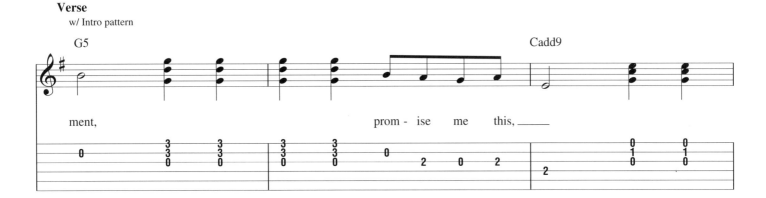

ment, prom - ise me this, _____

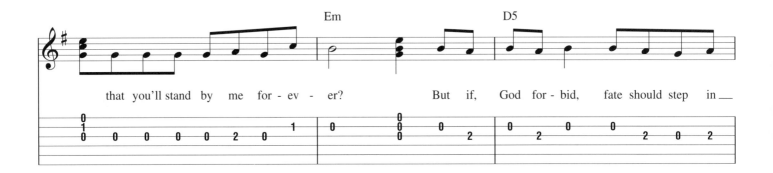

that you'll stand by me for - ev - er? But if, God for - bid, fate should step in ___

___ and force us in - to a good - bye,

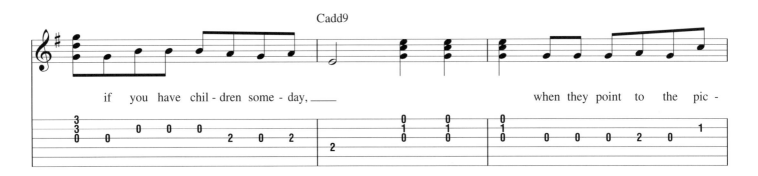

if you have chil - dren some - day, ___ when they point to the pic -

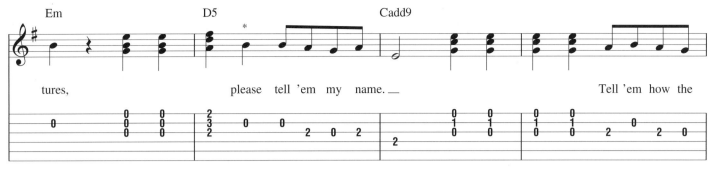

tures,   please tell 'em my name. ___   Tell 'em how the

*Sung one octave higher till end.

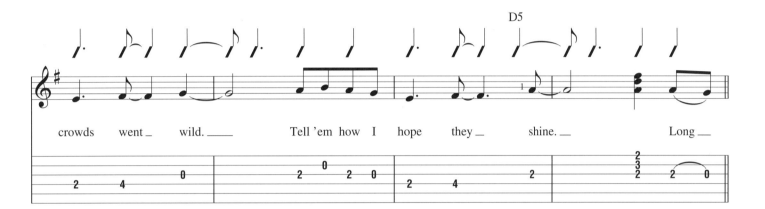

crowds   went _ wild. ___   Tell 'em how I hope they _   shine. ___   Long _

D.S. al Coda
(take 2nd ending)

Chorus

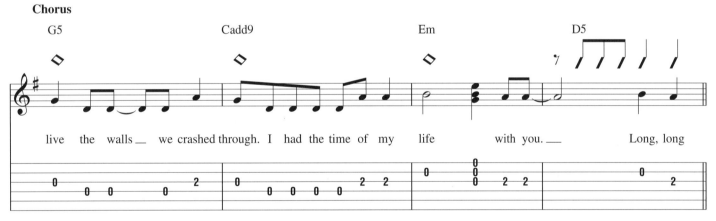

live   the walls _ we crashed through. I had the time of my   life   with you. ___   Long, long

Coda

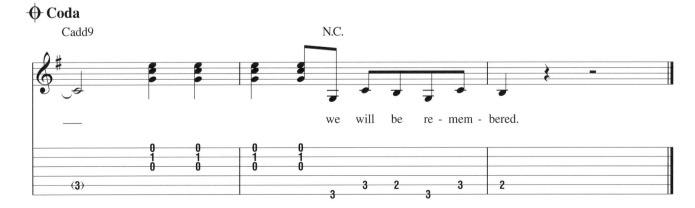

___   we   will   be   re - mem - bered.

Better than Revenge

Words and Music by Taylor Swift

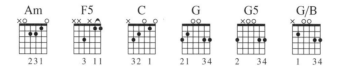

*Capo II

Strum Pattern: 1
Pick Pattern: 2

Intro
Moderately

*Optional: To match recording, place capo at 2nd fret.

Verse

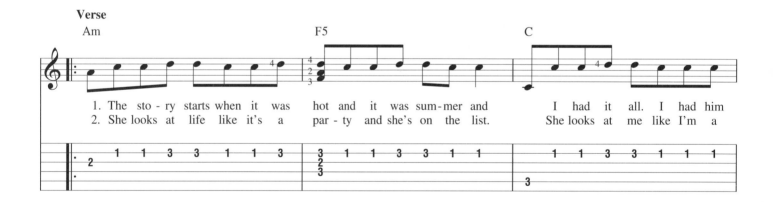

1. The sto - ry starts when it was hot and it was sum - mer and I had it all. I had him
2. She looks at life like it's a par - ty and she's on the list. She looks at me like I'm a

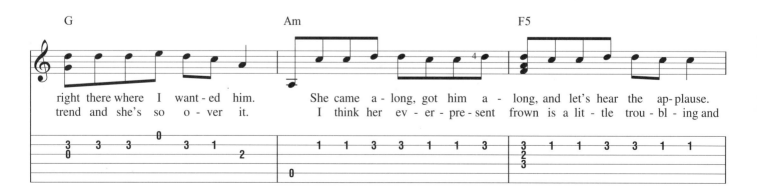

right there where I want - ed him. She came a - long, got him a - long, and let's hear the ap - plause.
trend and she's so o - ver it. I think her ev - er - pre - sent frown is a li - tle trou - bl - ing and

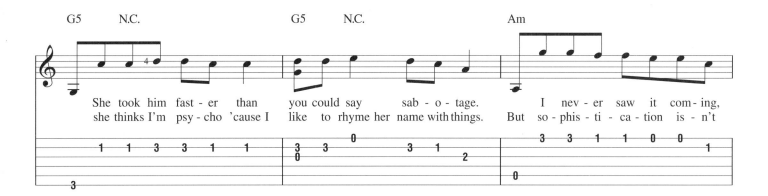

She took him fast-er than you could say sab-o-tage. I nev-er saw it com-ing,
she thinks I'm psy-cho 'cause I like to rhyme her name with things. But so-phis-ti-ca-tion isn't

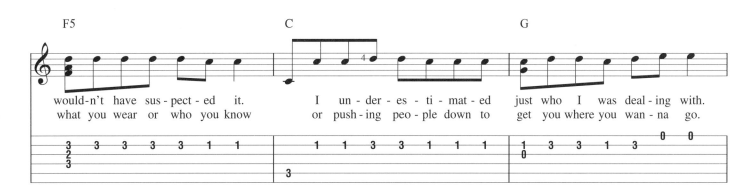

would-n't have sus-pect-ed it. I un-der-es-ti-mat-ed just who I was deal-ing with.
what you wear or who you know or push-ing peo-ple down to get you where you wan-na go.

She had to know the pain was beat-ing on me like a drum. She un-der-es-ti-mat-ed
They did-n't teach you that in prep school, so it's up to me, that no a-mount of vin-tage

𝄋 **Chorus**

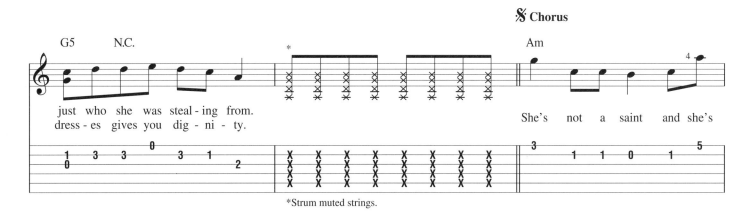

just who she was steal-ing from. She's not a saint and she's
dress-es gives you dig-ni-ty.

*Strum muted strings.

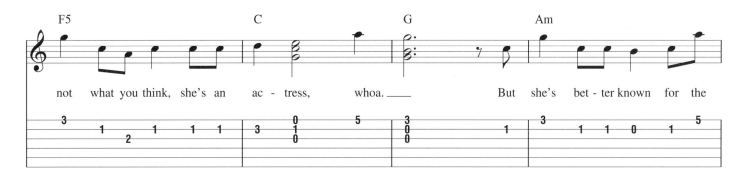

not what you think, she's an ac-tress, whoa. _____ But she's bet-ter known for the

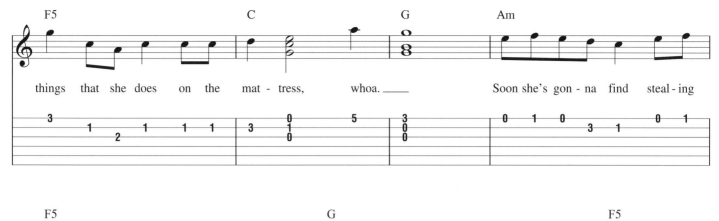

things that she does on the mat - tress, whoa. _____ Soon she's gon - na find steal - ing

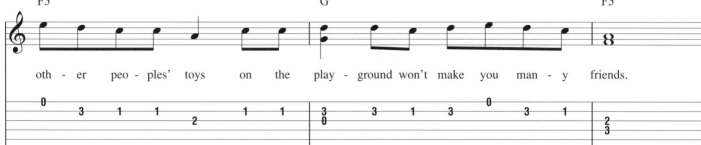

oth - er peo - ples' toys on the play - ground won't make you man - y friends.

To Coda ⊕

She should keep in mind, she should keep in mind there is noth - ing I do bet - ter than re - venge. _

*1st & 2nd times, let chord ring.

1.

Interlude

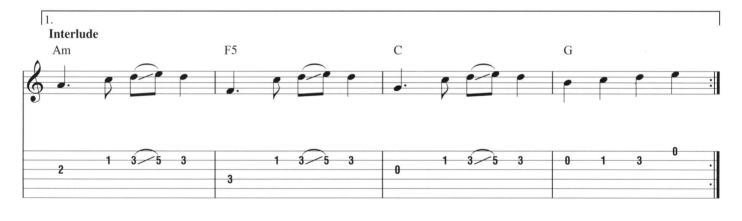

2.

Bridge

I'm just an - oth - er thing for you to roll your eyes at, hon - ey. You

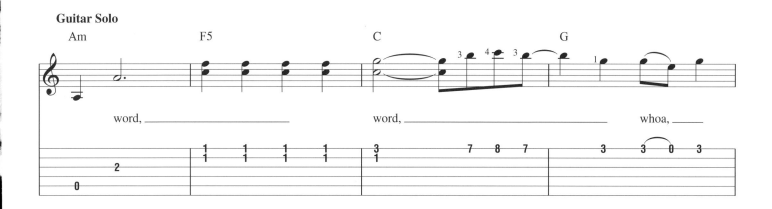

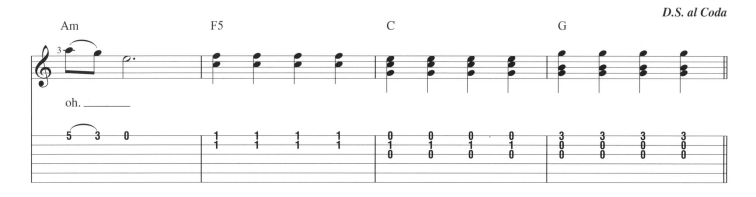

I don't think you do. Oh, ___ do you still feel like you

know what you're do - in'? I don't think you do, ___ I don't think you do. Let's hear the ap - plause. ___

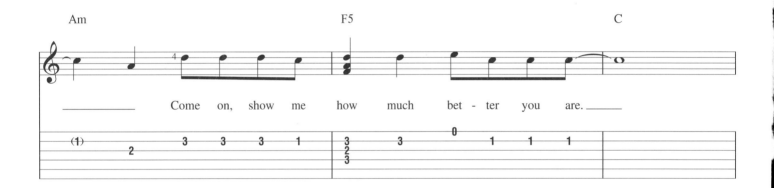

___ Come on, show me how much bet - ter you are. ___

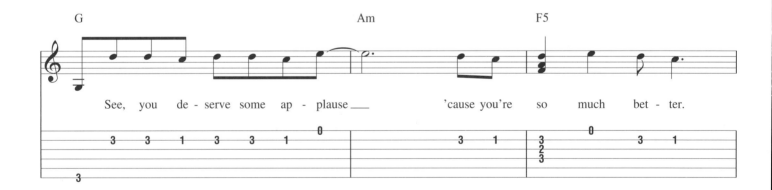

See, you de - serve some ap - plause ___ 'cause you're so much bet - ter.

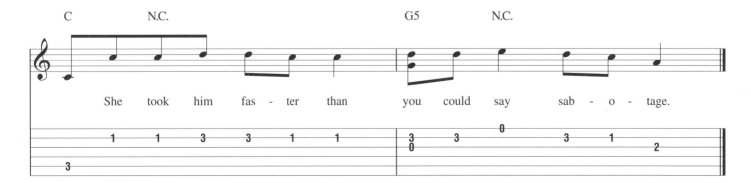

She took him fas - ter than you could say sab - o - tage.